Is That My Child? The Brain Food Plan

Help your child reach their potential and overcome learning difficulties

DR ROBIN PAUC

WITH CARINA NORRIS

First published in Great Britain in 2007 by
Virgin Books Ltd
Thames Wharf Studios
Rainville Road
London
W6 9HA

ISBN 978 07535 12951

The paper used in this book is a natural, recyclable product made from
wood grown in sustainable forests. The manufacturing process conforms to the
regulations of the country of origin.

Illustrations courtesy of: Kelly Brunt pages 22, 37 and Oxford

Typeset by Phoenix Photosetting, Chatham, Kent

CONTENTS

INTRODUCTION

In my first book on child learning difficulties *Is That My Child?* I stated that it was my opinion that dyslexia, dyspraxia, attention deficit disorder, attention deficit hyperactivity disorder, obsessive-compulsive disorder and Tourette's syndrome of childhood *do not* exist. That is, they do not exist in isolation, as they are symptoms and not conditions in their own right. They are also symptoms that will always appear in combination. This bold statement upset a few parents. However, the vast majority of parents that subsequently contacted me did so because they could identify with what I was saying and saw their child within the covers of that book.

The second thing the book did was to bring to the fore the concept of bpoptosis. Bpoptosis is the name I gave to the process during which a second wave of brain cells develop, migrate and make contact with other brain cells. This event principally takes place some four months after birth, and until the creation of this new word and its subsequent publication, the significance of this event and its involvement in the generation of symptom patterns in developmental delay had not been considered. Professor John Allman has related the absence of certain of these second-wave brain cells to true autism but it is my belief that this truly amazing event, which has been overlooked until now, is the fundamental underlying cause of developmental delay.

The treatment regime I advocate is a combination of diet, supplementation of omega-3 and omega-6 essential fatty acids, general and specific exercises designed to stimulate areas of the brain into action, and computer-generated programmes to follow on from this. Of these four crucial elements, the dietary changes have generated the most interest and have caused some confusion. Some people have taken things to the extreme, providing their child with an almost Atkins-type high-protein ultra-low carbohydrate diet, and have had to have the logic behind the dietary changes explained further. Others have struggled to implement the changes at all. It would seem that such events as Christmas, being on holiday or visiting relatives cause common sense to go out the window, together with all the benefits the child has gained.

I am delighted to have been able to join forces with Carina Norris, the nutritionist and author of numerous books including *You Are What You Eat: the meal planner that will change your life,* and the academic brains behind the nutrition plans for Channel 4's *Turn Back Your Body Clock.* Together I hope we will be able not only to provide continuing dietary advice for those children with developmental delay, but also to help *all* children establish a healthy diet for life. With increasing concern over the number of children who are clinically obese and poorly nourished, there has never been a better time than now to put in place *a diet for life.*

The second area of interest that has generated endless emails and phone calls concerned exercises; specifically, those we provide at the Tinsley House Treatment Centres. Before deciding to include these exercises in this book it was necessary to think long and hard, as some of the exercises are designed to be specifically 'left' or 'right' in terms of the effect they have on the central nervous system. Now, the majority of children visiting the clinics will have problems with the back of the brain on the left and the front of the brain on the right. However, as a tiny minority of children will have the exact opposite problem, some way of working out which is which is required. Generally it is the job of an experienced practitioner to do just that but, providing a series of simple tests are completed and the results of these tests are clear, I would suggest that the exercises in this book can be carried out on a daily basis in a graded fashion. If the tests are not clear or your child does not show signs of improvement over a period of a few weeks, an appointment should be made for an assessment by an experienced practitioner. With these provisos, we have included advice on general physical exercise, non-specific exercises designed to challenge the back of the brain, and exercises designed specifically to challenge areas of the brain on the right or the left.

Another area of concern has been with regard to supplementation of diet with omega-3 and omega-6 essential fatty acids and, more specifically, what dosage should be given, which brand to give and what to do if your child cannot or simply will not swallow the capsules or down the liquid. We have some good advice to help with this but have also decided it is necessary to provide a warning concerning certain products targeted specifically at children that contain artificial sweeteners, notably aspartame. A lot of research has been directed towards the effects of adding zinc sulphate as a supplement together with omegas-3 and -6 or in its own right as an alternative to such medication as Ritalin. As many parents are unsure whether or not to add zinc sulphate to their child's diet, we will look at this subject in a little more depth.

We will not consider in any detail the computer-generated programmes provided by the treatment centres as these can only be provided after the child has been tested by an experienced practitioner, and some have to be tailored to the individual child's needs.

This book should be a welcome companion volume to *Is That My Child?* It provides further dietary advice to the parents of the one in five children with learning or behavioural problems, together with advice on the need for adequate sleep, general physical exercise and specific brain-type exercises that can be carried out at home on a daily basis.

However, it is also a means whereby *every* parent can ensure their child is getting the best nutrition, adequate rest and sufficient exercise for optimum health, so they not only survive, but reach their highest possible level of personal achievement. To this end we will not only consider such topics as 'Increasing the brain fats' and 'Eating for balanced blood sugar' but also provide the skills necessary to read food labels and make you at least aware of the loopholes in the law that allow manufacturers to avoid telling the truth, the whole truth and nothing but the truth.

Robin Pauc

ABOUT THIS BOOK

This book aims to provide parents of all children – not only those diagnosed with a learning or behavioural problem – with information to help give them the best start in life through a healthy balanced diet, activity and exercise.

You'll find:

- Essential information on children's diets, concentrating on the nutrients that affect the brain's development and function
- A 14-day 'brain diet' to get you started
- Tips and ideas to help you build on the diet, the recipes included in the diet plan, plus useful extra recipes for building on the plan
- Physical exercises for all children, to keep them fit and active
- Brain exercises designed for children with learning and behavioural difficulties
- A 'workbook' section to help you plan your child's diet and exercise, and chart their progress

1

BEHAVIOUR AND LEARNING DIFFICULTIES

In the UK as many as one in five children find life difficult at home and in the classroom because of learning and behavioural problems. But whether a child has received one of the plethora of diagnoses for different kinds of learning and behavioural problems or not, I am convinced from my years of pioneering work at the Tinsley House Clinic that *all* children can benefit from the healthy 'brain-boosting' diet we have been using so successfully.

The right food is absolutely vital in helping your child's brain to develop properly. Good foods will support the brain, helping it to develop in the way that it should. Bad foods will harm the brain and stop it from doing its job properly. One of the clinic's starting points for the treatment of all children with learning and behavioural difficulties is to alter their diet to exclude harmful foods and replace them with beneficial foods.

In the past, children who struggled at school were simply labelled 'lazy', 'slow' or 'stupid', but in today's more enlightened times there are specific diagnoses for a wide range of problems. Foremost among these are attention deficit hyperactivity disorder (ADHD), attention deficit disorder (ADD), dyslexia, dyspraxia, obsessive-compulsive disorder (OCD), autism and Tourette's syndrome of childhood.

These children's distressing symptoms hold them back, preventing them from learning and stopping them from reaching their full potential, both in terms of academic achievement and learning to make friends and relate to other people. This is a huge concern to their parents, their teachers, and worst of all for the children themselves, who are not living their lives as happily as they could.

> Our special diet can help any child's behaviour and learning ability.

On top of the large number of children with learning difficulties (based on the 2001 census I estimate there are potentially more than two and a quarter million in the UK) there is an even larger number of children who exhibit milder symptoms that nevertheless hamper their performance at school, and their interactions with others. Perhaps they are extremely fidgety, boisterous, or find it very difficult to concentrate in class. There are probably very few parents who wouldn't recognise *any* behavioural or learning-related symptoms in their child, at least some of the time.

But isn't this simply children being children? Shouldn't we just accept a little bit of 'naughtiness' in a child, rather than attempting to 'medicalise' their condition, giving them a problem where none really exists?

I believe the answer is no. A lot of this kind of 'exuberant' behaviour (as opposed to the diagnosed conditions listed above) has become accepted as 'normal'. But it doesn't have to be. By making changes to your child's diet and routine, some of their problems can simply melt away – and this book will show you how.

Pigeonholing is not the solution

Today, 'labels' for behavioural and learning difficulties are universally used and many people find them useful. Many parents are relieved when they are told their child has dyslexia, ADHD or another of the learning or behaviour conditions – it reassures them that their child is not merely 'naughty' or 'stupid'. Also, with a diagnosis of a 'real' condition, they feel encouraged that treatment is possible and a solution is in sight. And crucially, the help and support given to a child depends upon their being diagnosed and labelled by the education and medical systems. A major comfort provided by labelling is the fact that when children are 'statemented' by the education system, they receive extra help at school. This reassures parents because they feel the burden is not theirs alone, and it helps teachers who find it difficult to give one child (or perhaps more) extra attention when they have a full classroom.

I believe, however, that these misleading labels should be replaced by the general term Developmental Delay. However, many teachers and parents fear (understandably) that if we take away these labels then we also take away children's hard-won entitlement to help and support in the classroom.

My opinion is that, although these conditions do not exist as separate conditions, these children do still have a need that should be addressed and they should receive backup in the form of statementing.

At Tinsley House we may not be the first to believe that the labels used to describe learning and behavioural difficulties are not only confusing but of little use or value, but we *are* the first to put forward a logical, scientific argument as to *why*. The most significant reason that these labels are not useful is that all of the conditions named above are *symptoms* of a wider underlying problem rather than *conditions* in their own right. We should treat the underlying cause, rather than simply concentrating on the symptoms. My new way of looking at these symptoms led to our effective treatment programme that radically transforms the lives of the children who undergo it.

The real root of the problem is a delay in the brain maturing (this will be explained in more detail in Chapter 3). This immature brain can't function properly, producing the symptoms of ADHD, ADD, dyslexia, etc. I would mention here that I use the term Developmental Delay Syndrome to describe all of these learning and behavioural difficulties (for reasons that will be explained later). So the treatment at Tinsley House Clinic is focused on helping the child's brain to develop properly.

The conditions never occur alone

The symptoms (not 'conditions') of dyslexia, dyspraxia, ADD, ADHD, OCD and Tourette's syndrome of childhood always occur together – a child will *always* have more than one of them, but to different degrees, and they will affect different children in different ways. If a child is correctly assessed and examined, this will be apparent, but many practitioners will fixate on the most obvious symptom to the exclusion of the others.

Crucially, your child's symptoms – and the degree to which they show them – provide the first step towards finding an effective treatment. Symptoms help a neurologist pinpoint where in the child's brain the problem lies and therefore which part of the brain needs help.

Now that we have a better handle on the problem we can treat the brain by supporting it (through simple exercises) and nourishing it (with the right food and supplements).

THE CONDITIONS – THE CURRENT SITUATION

At present when children are diagnosed with a behavioural or learning difficulty they are pigeonholed. Here I will briefly describe all of these learning and behavioural difficulties by their commonly used names; as I have explained, I personally use the term Developmental Delay Syndrome (DDS) for all of them.

Because I believe all learning difficulties are caused by a problem in the development of certain brain cells, all children with a learning difficulty will experience more than one condition. This may sound alarming, but the more we understand that this is the case, the easier it is to treat *all* the conditions.

Dyslexia
Dyslexia is defined as the impaired ability to read, spell and write words, despite the ability to see and recognise letters.

It can include various symptoms.

Delayed speech
The generally accepted rule of thumb of 'normal' development is to expect a child to use single words in the first year, two words together during the second year and mini-sentences in the third year.

Stuttering
Early onset stuttering – that is, more or less from when your child first starts to construct sentences – is not uncommon. The act of constructing a sentence takes place in the left side of the brain. The gaps

between words and the lilt of language is a right-brain activity. In fact 98 per cent of children with learning difficulties have problems predominantly in the right side of the brain and it is probably a delay in maturation here that causes this problem.

Recurrent ear infections, etc.

Glue ear, eczema and asthma are so common in association with learning and behavioural problems that they could be classed as a symptom. Again, this points to a problem on the right side of the brain, as part of the control mechanism for the immune system lives there.

Poor co-ordination

Although this is often included in the broad definition of dyslexia, poor co-ordination is in reality labelled dyspraxia, which I will discuss later.

Confusion over left- and right-handedness

In theory the left side of the brain should mature first, and this is thought to be why most people are right-handed (the left part of the brain controls the right side of the body in this case). There is a wave of special brain cells (including spindle cells) that develops in humans four months after birth. They are present on both sides of the brain but are concentrated on the right side, so can spur on left-handedness if there has been any delay in development of the brain up to this point. This can easily lead to confusion and the child ends up not sure which is left and which is right, and/or which hand to use.

Difficulty reading and/or the letters appearing to move on the page

In a recent study, 58 per cent of children attending my clinic were found to have accommodation/convergence failure. If you have to look at something close-up, as when reading, your eyes have to move inwards towards your nose so you can focus on the words. In most children with learning or behavioural difficulties, the left eye fails to do this. This not only causes problems for the brain in terms of processing the information that should be coming from both eyes, it also makes tracking across the page very difficult, often leading to what is called nystagmus. Interestingly, very few opticians test for convergence failure, which is something of a concern when so many children have this problem. Apart from this, a significant number of children have poor vision on testing, which rapidly improves once the brain's developmental delay is addressed.

YOU CAN TEST FOR CONVERGENCE YOURSELF

Take a pencil in your right hand and hold it up vertically, level with your child's eyes and roughly eighteen inches in front of them. Move it slowly towards your child's nose, telling them to look at it all the time. The eyes should start to move in at the same time and should be able to continue looking at the pencil even when it is only a few inches away from the nose. A delay in either eye starting to move in or an eye that moves out to the side while the pencil is still close to the nose is a sign of accommodation/convergence failure.

Light sensitivity
A small percentage of children diagnosed with dyslexia are hypersensitive to light – just a quick flash of light into the eyes during an examination causes the eyes to stream. This is generally a brainstem problem that runs in tandem with delayed development of the brain.

Co-existing conditions
Various forms of dyspraxia are often lumped in with dyslexia. Research has shown that 40 per cent of children with dyslexia also have attention deficit disorder (ADD) and/or attention deficit hyperactivity disorder (ADHD). We will see shortly that ADD and ADHD are also closely associated with other forms of behavioural problems.

Dyspraxia
Dyspraxia is defined as a partial loss of the ability to perform co-ordinated acts. It is an inability or difficulty in planning movements and carrying out planned movements or in orientating yourself within your environment. For children this means that daily tasks like

tying shoelaces and feeding themselves, and fun things like riding a bike, are enormous challenges. Not knowing exactly where you are in space means you constantly bump into things or drop things.

In the context of learning and behavioural disabilities, the term developmental dyspraxia should be used to cover the signs and symptoms that occur in these young children. The condition includes:

- Poor balance
- Difficulties in both fine (such as writing and painting) and gross (such as running and jumping) motor skills
- Problems with vision
- Problems with motor planning and perception, i.e. preparing a movement and awareness of where you are in space
- Poor bodily awareness
- Difficulty with reading, writing and speech
- Poor social skills
- Emotional/behavioural problems

Already we can see an intriguing overlap between developmental dyspraxia and dyslexia as described above. In a recent study completed at Tinsley House Clinic it was found that every child included in the study had varying degrees of developmental dyspraxia, regardless of the initial primary diagnosis – dyslexia, ADD, ADHD, OCD or Tourette's syndrome of childhood.

It is the right side of the brain that deals with your position in space and it is this side of the brain that shows developmental delay in nearly all (98 per cent) children with problems.

ADHD and ADD

In parallel with the emergence of dyslexia and dyspraxia, there is ADD and ADHD to contend with. These two conditions are an inability to concentrate on the job at hand or an inability to concentrate, combined with a tendency for the individual to cause disruption to their environment, due to an inability to remain still for more than a few seconds. We will look at the conditions separately.

Attention deficit hyperactivity disorder (ADHD)
This condition is poorly understood and it has been given three distinct subtypes to cover the various forms it may take.

To be diagnosed as ADHD, the symptoms must have been present for more than six months, be inappropriate for the child's age and intelligence, have developed before the age of seven, and have a negative impact in at least two social settings – home and school, for instance. The symptoms of ADHD fall into three main categories – hyperactivity, impulsivity and inattention.

Hyperactivity

This is an inability to sit still: constant foot-tapping and fidgeting, disruptive behaviour in the classroom, excessive talking, and an inability to do anything quietly are typical examples. The child will often act in a silly childish way, is attention-seeking, rough with their own and others' toys, and unfortunately often ends up hurting other children.

Impulsivity

This can be in both communication and actions. The child will attempt to answer questions before they are completed, almost desperate to be the first to answer, or will interrupt conversations with inappropriate questions. The child cannot wait for their turn, intrudes into others' play and tends to have a short fuse and erupts, lashing out, when frustrated.

Inattention

Though the two conditions overlap, the 'inability to pay attention' aspect of ADHD not surprisingly provides an accurate description of what is categorised as ADD, and the conditions are often said to co-exist. Examples of such inattention can be: having a poor attention span, making silly mistakes, not completing tasks, not appearing to be listening, being easily distracted, having a poor short-term memory and avoiding anything that involves a sustained mental effort.

Children with developmental delay invariably suffer from low self-esteem and this is often present in children with ADHD symptoms, which should not be missed even though outwardly they seem fairly robust. The frustration that can lead to violent outbursts is a clear sign of the hopelessness many of these children feel but cannot express.

With ADHD in particular, there is also another very worrying aspect that the parent may not only fail to recognise, but unwittingly panders to. Many of these children are carbohydrate addicts, sugar junkies, surviving on a diet high in carbohydrates and little else.

Just as dyslexia impacts on a child's learning, children with symptoms predominantly of ADHD may suffer difficulties, due to the hyperactivity and poor ability to concentrate. They often suffer from low self-esteem, get into trouble and live in a world they cannot understand.

Clearly these children will not get the best from the education that is provided for them, but unfortunately neither will the other children in the classroom, as the disruptive behaviour and the need for extra supervision by teaching staff to manage the overactive child leaves the others disadvantaged. 'Disruptive' children often end up excluded from school and their parents are faced with a struggle to find a school place for them.

Attention deficit disorder (ADD)

ADD is a term used to describe a child who has difficulty focusing and maintaining attention. A child must exhibit six or more of the following diagnostic criteria to be considered as suffering from ADD:

- Often fails to pay attention to detail and makes careless mistakes
- Often has difficulty sustaining attention
- Often does not seem to listen
- Often fails to complete work
- Often has problems with organisation
- Often avoids/dislikes tasks that involve mental effort
- Often loses things
- Is easily distracted
- Is often forgetful

The child with ADD generally behaves like any other child – misbehaving, being silly and daydreaming – the only difference being the constant and extreme nature of the behaviour pattern. When the child's behaviour impacts upon family life and schooling, it can be judged to be a problem.

In general, the word to best describe ADD is distractibility. ADD children are distracted by any environmental stimulus and almost appear to be looking for anything that will give them cause to put aside the task set before them.

The other aspects often associated with ADD again point to the fact that it is a symptom of developmental delay and not a cause in itself. Impulsivity, hyperactivity, clumsiness, mood swings and poor social skills have all been closely associated with ADD. If we were to replace those behavioural traits with known conditions the sentence would read – ADHD and dyspraxia. The physical cause of this is, in fact, an under-functioning prefrontal cortex.

Obsessive-compulsive disorder (OCD)

Obsessive-compulsive disorder is defined as a condition marked by a compulsion to perform certain acts repetitively or carry out certain rituals. It is characterised by obsessional traits, and may present simply as a need in the child to place certain objects in a preordained order. At the other extreme it is a condition that can dominate the child's life, where order and routines make normal everyday life unbearable or unlivable.

Washing, checking and ordering rituals are particularly common in children. In childhood OCD is subtle, as in play, when toy cars have to be placed in a particular order, or dressing, when certain items have to be put on first. OCD is often associated with anxiety and depression but is particularly related to Tourette's syndrome.

Tourette's syndrome of childhood

Tourette's syndrome is defined as a rare form of generalised tic usually beginning in childhood, between two and fifteen years of age, and marked by uncontrolled continuous gestures, facial twitching, foul language and repetition of sentences spoken by other persons. It would appear that more and more children are manifesting tics and subtle signs of Tourette's, perhaps no more than a frequent clearing of the throat, blinking, grunting or facial grimacing.

Far from being rare, researchers now consider aspects of tics to be evident in virtually all children at some point as the brain grows and matures. Often the signs are so subtle that even parents aren't aware their child is showing signs of Tourette's along with the more obvious aspects of dyspraxia, ADHD and OCD that may be happening at the same time.

But aren't these all signs that parents sometimes see in an over-tired or anxious child? Well, yes, the repetition of words or sentences is something we all do as a learning process – it is only when the symptoms increase and persist that concerns should be raised. The use of bad language is part of a caricature of Tourette's and is actually pretty rare. Tourette's syndrome of childhood is currently said to afflict one child in every hundred.

A child with OCD or Tourette's syndrome may suffer an almost intolerable daily turmoil, a misery often only shared with a parent, as they struggle with the compulsions that they can in part control but ultimately must give in to. These children not only suffer from low self-esteem but also terrible frustrations and inner sadness, often made worse by tactless comments.

Autism

An alternative name for the 'autistic spectrum' is pervasive developmental disorder, and this would fit in quite well within my proposed new classification of Developmental Delay Syndrome. The three key symptoms for autistic spectrum disorders include poor development of social skills, communication and imagination, but may also occur in association with dyslexia, ADD and ADHD.

All the subgroups of autism suggested to date, including Asperger's syndrome, overlap, and the boundaries are unclear. However, in reality, if you examine a patient with 'typical autism' – that is, a patient with autistic tendencies – you will find aspects of dyspraxia, dyslexia, ADD, ADHD or OCD.

The presentation of autism varies widely and many individuals with more severe forms have identifiable underlying medical conditions including a variety of congenital, chromosomal and metabolic diseases. It has now been suggested by Professor John Allman that *true* autism is due to the *absence* of the brain's spindle cells. In other words, the spindle cells among the second wave of brain cells that develop four months after birth are either not produced or else they die. Because of this, true autism is not responsive to the form of treatment offered at Tinsley House.

Checking and monitoring for improvements

An important part of the treatment we provide is monitoring progress. We need to document all signs of improvement and gather this information from various sources. Usually the parents are the first to comment on the little things they have noticed, but this is quickly followed by reports from other significant people in the child's life, including relatives, friends of the family and school-teachers.

The subjective findings are provided by constant reassessment, with the child being retested at each visit and also between treatments. This constant monitoring not only allows the practitioner to see how the child is progressing, but is a great encouragement to the parents.

The best measure of all has to be when children tell me how well they are coping, how well they are doing at school and how different they are feeling. Little else really matters.

2

HELPING YOUR CHILD

Does my child need help?

All children are different. They develop at different rates, and it can be difficult for parents to decide whether their child is simply lagging behind a little bit, or whether they have a problem that should be addressed.

If a child *does* have a Developmental Delay Syndrome (DDS), the sooner the problem receives attention, the better. Ideally, this will be before the child begins school. Left untreated, they will struggle to keep up with their classmates, probably leading to low self-esteem – no one likes to be bottom of the class.

But even if a DDS isn't diagnosed until much later, it's not too late to make changes that can help.

Without a proper consultation, it's not possible to categorically decide that a child does or does not have a DDS. However, there are several factors, events and behaviours, which parents may recognise in their own offspring, that can strongly suggest that it is in fact a DDS that is causing their child's difficulties.

Risk factors for Developmental Delay Syndromes

Several factors increase the risk of Developmental Delay Syndromes in a child.

Family history, pregnancy and birth:

- A family history of learning difficulties
- A 'problematic' pregnancy for the mother
- Premature birth
- Assisted delivery (ventouse, Caesarean or forceps) rather than natural delivery
- Foetal distress at the birth

The early days:

- A child who did not crawl
- A child who did not walk until after one year old
- A child who did not develop a vocabulary of single words during their first year
- A child who did not learn to put two words together during their second year
- A child who could not manage mini-sentences by their third year

Toilet matters:

- A child who is not potty-trained until older than two-and-a-half years
- A child who wets the bed after the age of three years
- A child who has soiled themselves

Reading, writing and learning:

- A child who has problems with reading and writing
- A child who has difficulty concentrating
- A child who is hyperactive
- A child with a poor short-term memory

Other behaviour:

- A child who has displayed rituals and/or obsessions

- A child who has displayed involuntary movements, tics, excessive blinking, grimacing, or made repeated sounds
- A clumsy or accident-prone child

The symptoms that present themselves will depend on where in the brain the problem lies and the pattern of symptoms this will produce. So I have suggested four clearly identifiable sub-classifications that may help you to grasp the new concept.

Developmental Delay Syndrome – dyslexic type:

- Dyslexia is the predominant feature

Developmental Delay Syndrome – cerebellar type:

- Dyspraxia is the predominant feature

Developmental Delay Syndrome – Tourette's/OCD/ADHD type:

- Tics or obsessive behaviour are prominent features

Developmental Delay Syndrome – pervasive type:

- Autistic tendencies are present

I believe that having redefined these problems, and realised that all of the common learning difficulties are symptoms of an underlying immaturity of the brain, we have taken a huge step forward in our understanding of what is happening, but have not as yet explained the cause of the underlying malfunction.

The good news

Learning that your child has a DDS is, in fact, good news – because once we know what the problem is, we can begin treating it. And it's important to remember that the brain's development is simply *delayed*, not permanently damaged. By combining a programme of putting the child on a healthier diet, and stimulating the brain through both mental and physical exercises, I have seen remarkable improvements in every child I've treated. Most often, their symptoms have disappeared entirely. The same can be done for your child – and that is where this book can help.

3

BRAIN SCIENCE FOR BEGINNERS

In order to understand how the Tinsley House Clinic treatment helps children with Developmental Delay Syndrome, it's necessary to learn a little about the brain. Once we know how the brain develops normally, we can compare this with what happens in DDS, and understand how the special brain-stimulating exercises and healthy diet help children to 'catch up' and achieve their full potential. The crucial piece of the jigsaw puzzle that has been missing until the publication of the work at Tinsley House was the fact that some four months after birth a second wave of brain cells develop and migrate, and it is the areas of brain where these cells end up that are central to the generation of the symptoms of DDS.

One of these areas is called the anterior cingulate and lies on the medial (inside) wall of the brain in the prefrontal cortex. When this area of the brain under-functions, the typical signs of ADD/ADHD will appear. Although spindle cells have been known about for years it is only in the last few years that researchers such as Professors John Allman and Ester Nimchinsky have looked again at these cells that truly define our humanity. Recently spindle cells have been renamed and are now known as von Economo neurons in honour of their discoverer.

Because the significance of this truly amazing event has been totally overlooked until now, I felt it necessary to provide a new word to describe the development, migration and maturation of these second-wave brain cells and so the word bpoptosis was born.

Below the main part of the brain and on top of the brainstem sits a 'little brain', the cerebellum, which can be thought of as the computer that drives the brain. Both the brain and the cerebellum are divided into two sides, called hemispheres – 'cerebral hemispheres' for the brain, and 'cerebellar hemispheres' for the cerebellum – the right cerebellar hemisphere drives the left cerebral hemisphere, and vice versa. This means that if, for example, there is a problem with the right cerebellar hemisphere, there will also be problems with the functions normally performed by the left cerebral hemisphere.

The brainstem and cerebellum are responsible for what is called temporal sequencing – basically, setting a time frame for motor activity (movements) and co-ordinating and sequencing the movements of the two sides of the body.

If there is a problem with the communication between the cerebellum and brainstem, and the brain, we will see symptoms of dyspraxia. And other desynchronisations of the brain's rhythm also cause numerous problems, manifesting themselves in many different ways and causing an apparent slowing of the brain's processing speed and thereby brain function.

View of Inside of the Right Hemisphere of the Brain

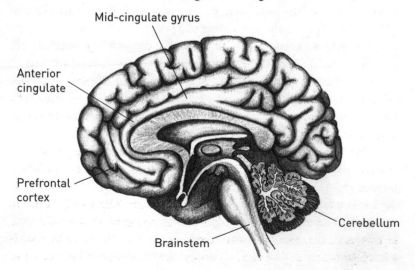

Mid-cingulate gyrus

Anterior cingulate

Prefrontal cortex

Cerebellum

Brainstem

How is this relevant to learning difficulties?

If we know which part of the brain is used for particular tasks, then we can start to make comparisons between how that part of the brain functions when a child is performing a task well and how it functions when the child is having difficulties with a task.

At Tinsley House Clinic we rely on eye, balance and other examinations to discover which part of the brain is experiencing problems. Locating and observing the area of the brain that is affected in each learning difficulty is the most revolutionary and exciting aspect of our work. This link had not been made by anyone before. As you can imagine, this has important ramifications for how a child should be treated.

We then considered whether if we stimulated the affected area of the brain we should see an improvement in the child's ability to do the relevant tasks. The results were very exciting, much more so than we could have imagined.

By further study of the brain, we also realised that the food children eat has a huge impact on the efficiency of brain function, and so the correct diet has to be a key part of the treatment.

WHAT IS DIFFERENT ABOUT THE BRAINS OF CHILDREN WITH DDS?

As humans have evolved, our brains have had to grow, and new pathways develop so the new parts can work. This is like a town that is growing in size – as it grows new roads have to be constructed to link the new areas to the old. With the brain, new connections are needed if the new and sophisticated parts are to be brought into use.

So the brain has expanded, developing ever-increasing quantities of neocortex (new brain) overlying the paleo- and archeocortex (old brain). The skull, too, has evolved and expanded over time to house and protect the delicate evolving brain tissue.

This is all very well, but we now come up against a problem – that of the bony pelvis and the birth canal in females. Ideally a human child should stay in the womb until at least 21 months, so the brain is sufficiently mature that at birth the child would soon be walking on its way to independence. But two problems would arise in this situation. Firstly, few mothers would be able to endure such a long gestation period and, secondly, the child would be much too big to be delivered. Nature's solution to the problem is to have the child delivered 'prematurely' at nine months, thus greatly extending the length of time when the child is totally dependent upon its parents.

If we compare a few developmental facts relating to a newborn chimpanzee and a newborn human baby we will see quite clearly how this strategy works. Although human babies and baby chimps both have approximately the same size brains at birth, their abilities are vastly different.

A chimp baby:

- Can walk one month after birth
- Has an adult brain at seven months
- Can lead a relatively independent life and survive alone if need be after seven months
- Has a brain that grows from 350cc at birth to 450cc

A human baby:

- Cannot walk until about one year
- Does not achieve a full-size adult brain for years – adolescence or later
- Requires an extended period of nurturing if it is to survive
- Has a brain that grows from 350cc at birth to 1400cc

From the above it would seem logical to assume that human babies are not ready to be born at nine months. Their brains are incomplete. Also, although humans have chimp-size brains at birth, our brains grow significantly larger. But more importantly, there is a difference in the numbers of certain types of brain cell. One of these types, spindle cells, have been known about for years, but only recently have I discovered their importance in human development.

The amazing spindle cells

Apart from humans, spindle cells are found only in the brains of animals we think of as being most like us – the great apes (orang-utans, gorillas, chimpanzees and bonobos, or pygmy chimps). In 2006 research was published stating that spindle cells are also to be found in the brains of whales. The significance of this is yet to be established but it would appear that spindle cells are more likely to be associated with larger brains, the ability to communicate and social behaviour. However, in terms of the quantity of spindle cells found in the great apes, orang-utans have only a few spindle cells in their brains; gorillas, chimps and bonobos have increasing numbers, but still not that many. By contrast, humans have tens of thousands of spindle cells.

It is the development of these spindle cells in the human brain at four months that makes us unlike other animals. It is only humans who suffer from learning and behavioural difficulties, so it makes sense to look at the brain cells that make us uniquely human. That is where the answer to developmental delay lies, in spindle cells.

Spindle cells are only found in a small area of the brain called the prefrontal cortex – the front of the brain. This area of the brain has been implicated in the guiding of attention, pain and fear, and also in modulating the workings of the autonomic nervous system, which controls all the things we don't think about like heart rate and blood pressure. Clearly, the fact that these cells are found in so few species must have special significance, especially when we consider that humans possess so many.

Spindle cells are crucial for us to function to our full potential in our highly structured society. An absence of spindle cells results in autism, while under-functioning spindle cells cause ADD and ADHD. Furthermore, all areas of the prefrontal cortex must work together for us to develop normally.

This is how it works:

1. The first wave of brain cells that develop while you are in the womb give you the potential for intelligence
2. The second wave of brain cells that develop at four months of age makes you human and gives you the ability to concentrate on what you are doing (for instance, to be able to sit still in class)

The key point here is that, even if you are a genius, if you can't concentrate you can't or won't learn properly. Children with developmental delay might appear to be not too bright because they struggle to read and write. But once their problem is addressed, they can catch up because the obstructions to their learning have been removed.

By the same token, having developmental delay treated won't necessarily turn a child into a genius if the potential wasn't there in the first place.

Having a developmental delay treated will improve your child's concentration and enable their ability to learn to progress. The right treatment will unleash their full potential and enable them to work towards achieving their goals in life. That surely is good news.

Why do only humans have DDS?

So why should humans be the only animals to suffer from DDS? This can be explained by simply taking into account two facts: the human baby's vulnerability to stressors, and low infant mortality rates among humans.

Vulnerability to stressors

Being born prematurely and therefore having an immature and incomplete brain makes us vulnerable to any stressor.

Stressors can include:

- The level of oestrogen in the mother's blood when she is pregnant
- Foetal distress at birth
- A diet containing additives and E numbers and too much salt and sugar
- A lack of certain essential fats

Genetics, family history and gender (DDS is more common in boys) may also be factors. The new science of epigenetics may provide the answer as to why certain stressors cause problems and why such things as changing what we eat can change our ability to learn as well as our behaviour. The epigenome is basically protein switches that can literally switch on and off genes. It is now considered quite possible that environmental cues can alter the epigenome and switch on or off genes that are not only responsible for the events that take place in our bodies – both good and bad – but also the timing of events that govern our development.

BOYS AT RISK

Could there be other causes of developmental delay other than genetics? Does the genome really play such a role? A clue to the answer to this came from looking at the sex bias occurring in developmental delay syndromes. The vast majority (70 per cent) of sufferers of developmental delay are boys. The cell development that takes place four months after birth can be delayed by genetic factors that come into play. Boys are more susceptible to these genetic weaknesses becoming active and the cell development being delayed, as they are more vulnerable to their mother's stress levels when developing in the womb.

It is thought that the male brain is vulnerable to the mother's oestrogen level and that any rise in her circulating level of oestrogen may affect a developing male brain when a developing female brain would have remained unaffected. The circulating oestrogen level can only exert this effect during a critical period of development. However, the fact remains that male brains are more vulnerable during development and remain so during the maturation process.

Also, although the female brain is smaller than the male brain, it is now known that certain critical areas of the female brain have a greater surface area and therefore greater functional capabilities. It is claimed that, due to this, the female brain is better suited to cope with the stresses of modern-day living, having greater endurance, coping strategies and multitasking capabilities.

Low infant mortality

Because humans nurture their offspring for so long (far longer than most other animals), the infant death rate falls. Natural selection is thus avoided and weak genes are perpetuated. In the wild an animal with even a minor genetic problem is unlikely to survive. This is not the case with humans, and so minor genetic problems (that do not affect our survival) can be passed on.

The role of genetics:

- If a child's mother has a defined developmental syndrome, the chance of genetic problems being passed on to one or more of her offspring are in the region of 32 per cent
- If a child's father has a defined developmental syndrome, this probability rises dramatically to more than 70 per cent

However, the fact that one or both parents have had developmental problems does not necessarily mean their offspring *will* be affected, just that the predisposition exists. The predisposition can become active – expressed – or as in the case of certain mice genetically destined to be fat and die of cancer/diabetes, turned off just by changing the diet.

The question remains: why do these problematic symptoms appear in the first place? We said earlier that Nature has had to come up with certain strategies to get round the problem of fitting a bigger, more sophisticated brain and skull through the female birth canal. The answer is to have the baby born prematurely (at nine months rather than twenty-one months, when the brain would be better developed) and then greatly extend the nurturing period required until the child can survive unaided.

Although the primitive brain is able to function, it takes time for the neocortex (new brain) to mature and then, and only then, exert a higher level of control over the older, primitive part of the brain. It is the variability in this process of maturation of the neocortex – some children taking longer than others – that generates the various symptoms of developmental delay. Without treatment these symptoms can persist for a lifetime. In other words, we will all demonstrate minor symptoms of developmental delay to some degree or another, but as the brain matures and the various areas catch up and level out in terms of function, these symptoms should disappear. However, if there is a genetic predisposition towards a developmental delay and this predisposition is brought into being by foetal distress, then the symptoms of developmental delay will appear and remain unless treated correctly.

A prime example of the varying maturity of the brain is in gaining control of the bladder. We all expect babies to have to wear nappies, but to gain control of their bladder at around two years – at first during the day, and then through the night. In terms of gaining bladder control, the frontal cortex has to develop and mature to a point where it can exert control over the more primitive regions of the nervous system. This development and maturity will vary from child to child, depending upon the various factors we have considered already.

The reason why night control comes after daytime continence is that at night the level of brain activity drops and so there is, in effect, less control; only when the brain has matured still further and the level of brain activity during sleep is sufficient, can a decision – to pee or not to pee – be made.

Controlling the emotions, and the social graces

Let us consider two similar situations with very different outcomes. In the first situation an adult wants to buy an expensive item; they consult their partner as it involves their joint incomes. The other partner agrees the purchase would be a good idea but suggests deferring the purchase for a month, by which time the bank balance should be a little healthier. Result: both partners are happy.

In the second situation a young child sees a doll and decides she wants it and wants it NOW. The mother explains to the child that she can't afford the doll this week but may be able to buy it at the end of the month. Result: a tantrum, and neither mother nor child are happy.

So what is the difference between these two situations? In the first scenario the partner had a mature adult brain and could cope with what is called 'deferred gratification'. In other words, you have to wait for what you want – you don't get it immediately. In the second scenario the child could not cope with this deferred gratification – hence the tantrum.

The basic problem here is time. In order to understand that you will get the doll, but not now, you require an understanding of words that relate to time – tomorrow, next week, soon. So to have any chance of understanding time your prefrontal cortex (the very front of the brain) needs to be functioning properly.

With all young children we expect problems like the one mentioned above – it is a normal part of growing up – but what if this were to continue well past the toddler stage? Now you have a real problem. Again, this is a clear sign that a part of the prefrontal cortex is delayed in its development.

LOOKING IN THE WRONG PLACE

Let's now look at what has been attempted in terms of treatment and why such treatments don't work.

In order to treat any condition you have to know just what is causing it. For example, a stomachache could just be the result of overindulging in a rich meal the night before, or it could be something more serious. So a stomachache is a *symptom* of an underlying problem, be it short term like overindulgence at the dinner table or long term. We don't say, 'Ah, I'm suffering from stomachache, that's a condition,' and leave it at that. If it persists, we investigate further to find the cause, so it can be treated and, hopefully, cured.

For years, researchers have been looking for a cause for dyslexia, but because they considered dyslexia a condition in its own right they were looking in the wrong place. Endless papers have been published, and geneticists have been trying to find a dyslexia gene. But how can they when dyslexia, as a condition, does not exist? It is like looking for a stomachache or headache gene when they are just symptoms of something else altogether.

Dyslexia symptoms

Treatments for dyslexia tend to fall into three distinct types – a variety of exercises, devices to help limit the visual problems associated with the condition, and educational strategies to help the child progress in spite of their affliction. Providing exercises to children with dyslexia that are specifically designed to stimulate the back part of the brain – the cerebellum – will most certainly help at first. However, without a clear understanding of what dyslexia is and what causes it – which leads to applying the correct treatment – they are bound to fail in the long run.

Similarly, providing glasses with coloured lenses or putting coloured overlays over the page will help, but they certainly will not be a permanent solution. In a recent study it was found that 58 per cent of children with developmental delay could not bring their eyes in towards the nose when viewing an object close up. If this problem is not addressed then it does not matter what you do in terms of coloured filters.

Dyspraxia symptoms

The treatments for dyspraxia are again based on exercise, which will help to some extent but cannot be a solution to the problem, as dyspraxia is never found on its own. Therefore, as with dyslexia, you have to treat the underlying cause, not just one of its signs.

ADHD symptoms

ADHD has been treated by a variety of approaches varying from behaviour management to diet (in the case of more enlightened practitioners), but ultimately vast numbers of children are managed by drug therapy. This can be remarkably effective and the answer to the prayers of parents who are at their wits' end, but controlling the child's behaviour using these drugs has come at a terrible cost. Evidence is now emerging that the use of drugs in the management of ADHD may cause long-term brain damage. If this proves to be true we must surely look at alternative methods. (Notice I used the word 'management', not 'treatment', because it is not a treatment – it only manages the ADHD.)

Tourette's syndrome and obsessive-compulsive disorder

Tourette's syndrome and OCD are so common in childhood as to be considered a 'normal' stage that nearly all children pass through. Clearly it is the degree of grimacing or indulging in rituals that is critical here in deciding whether there is a problem to be addressed. These signs and symptoms are caused by delays, by degree, in the maturation and functioning of various areas of the brain. If detected early enough they can be treated effectively and will, like the trivial signs observed in virtually every child, gradually fade away. However, unless we recognise the true situation – that is, the delay that can occur in the development of the brain that takes place four months after birth – then these early signs may be missed or mistreated. Again, any drug therapy offered will only manage the condition.

Hopefully, with the breakthrough made at Tinsley House Clinic as to the underlying cause and the understanding that these conditions are no more than symptoms, treatments can now be directed towards the real problem.

We have added together what was known and the discoveries I have made to offer a revolutionary new treatment for learning and behavioural difficulties. Some previous treatments have been close to realising that the problem lies in the brain, but because no one was looking in the right place they only got part of the way there. What works at the clinic is a bit like how you make a cake; by combining the right ingredients and putting them together in the correct way, you will get the right result.

The ingredients of the Tinsley House treatment are beautifully simple: a brain-supporting diet, supplementation with essential fatty acids, as far as possible the exclusion of bad E numbers and artificial sweeteners, and simple yet effective brain and eye stimulation exercises.

A solution for your child

Now that we have a new light on learning and behavioural difficulties at Tinsley House Clinic we are able to offer an effective, lasting and noninvasive treatment. We can locate the problem and do something about it. The parents and children who come here are delighted with the results.

Your child will need to be properly diagnosed for a full treatment programme to be prescribed. At the time of writing, there are only a handful of Tinsley House Treatment Centres that offer this programme, but I am hoping that others will be able to offer it soon (see www.tinsleyhouseclinic.com for news on that front). But you can start work today by working on your child's diet, and this book will show you how.

As the first step towards finding a solution we need to look at clinical manifestations – how the symptoms appear in the child – and relate them to the underlying problems in the child's brain.

Different areas of the central nervous system can under-function and, as a result, produce signs and symptoms (commonly labelled dyslexia, dyspraxia, ADD, ADHD, OCD or Tourette's syndrome in childhood) to varying degrees of severity. No two children will have exactly the same problems and therefore can only be diagnosed based on their unique mix of symptoms. *Children cannot be properly diagnosed by labelling them and then treating them only based on their main symptom.*

It is the dominance of a particular sign or symptom within a syndrome that often guides the practitioner towards the wrong diagnosis. I have yet to meet a child with only a single symptom and it is for this reason that it is so important to realise that a symptom is not a disorder. Regarding the predominant symptom as a condition in itself limits consideration of what the answer to the problem is. If you're only aware of part of the problem it will be difficult to find a solution.

How can we limit the factors involved in DDS?

So far we have looked at the various reasons why developmental delay syndromes can occur. It is clear that the premature birth strategy devised by Nature provides the underlying predisposition – and this is not preventable. Stress factors in the womb play a role, and these may eventually be preventable if we identify how to avoid this happening. Furthermore, the effects of birth intervention may be preventable depending on what can be done to change birthing practices. Genetics, to a degree, throws the final dice, and this may be preventable if future research shows which gene or genes are involved and what factors tweak the genome.

Given that these things are largely unavoidable at the current time our focus should be on being aware of them and discovering if there is anything we can do to limit either the onset or the effect once established.

I have mentioned the importance of good nutrition for children and this has to be the starting point either in 'prevention' or treatment. In fact, regardless of whether there is a developmental problem or not, the growing brain needs certain essential elements in the diet, not just to function but to grow, develop and fulfil its potential.

4

SPECIFIC EXERCISES AND PRACTICAL ADVICE

In *Is That My Child?* I made a conscious decision not to include specific brain type exercises. I felt at the time that as the exercises have to be tailored to the individual child's needs, and as this can only be decided upon following a series of tests that indicate the area of brain and side of brain needing stimulation, it could lead to a few children doing the wrong exercises. However, following a deluge of emails from around the world I have had to reconsider the situation and provide a structured series of exercises that can be carried out at home on a daily basis; these should accompany any dietary changes that have been put in place and the supplementation of omega-3 and -6.

GENERAL EXERCISES

The following exercises can be carried out by *any* child, regardless of whether they have learning and behavioural problems or not. Many children who are already very sporty and wish to excel in their chosen field have found the exercises to be very beneficial in helping to achieve better balance and hand-eye co-ordination. The first three exercises must be carried out *slowly* and continued until they can be done perfectly.

Exercise 1

With hands by the side, head in the neutral position and eyes closed, walk up and then down three stairs, three times, and repeat three times a day. Never go higher than three stairs. When you can do three repetitions perfectly, do five, then seven, then ten.

Exercise 2

Once you have mastered forward stair-walking, do it backwards with the same progressions.

Exercise 3

Once you can stair-walk forwards and backwards, start forward stair-walking again but this time carrying a tray with a plastic tumbler full of water on it.

Exercise 4

Rocker board – these can be used for younger children and should be used at least three times a day.

Exercise 5

Wobble boards – these can be used by any age group and for younger children can be used after the child has mastered the rocker board.

Exercise 6

Balance balls – these can be used by very young children, the parent holding the child's hands while moving them on the ball so that they lose and then regain balance. This must be done slowly.

NB, children must be supervised by a responsible adult at all times while carrying out these exercises.

SPECIFIC EXERCISES

Before attempting these exercises it is essential to carry out the series of simple tests that follow in order to establish which side of the body and hence the brain needs to be exercised. Following each test tick the appropriate box – Left or Right.

Test 1

Get your child to stand in front of you with feet together, hands by their side and eyes closed. Having told them what you are going to do, gently but firmly tap the upper arm just below shoulder level, firstly on the left, then on the right. Repeat this two or three times. Note if the child loses balance, moves a foot or an arm. Tick the box on page 41 for the side the child falls towards, or the opposite side to the foot or arm that moved. So if your child falls to the left, or the right arm or foot moves, you tick the *left* box.

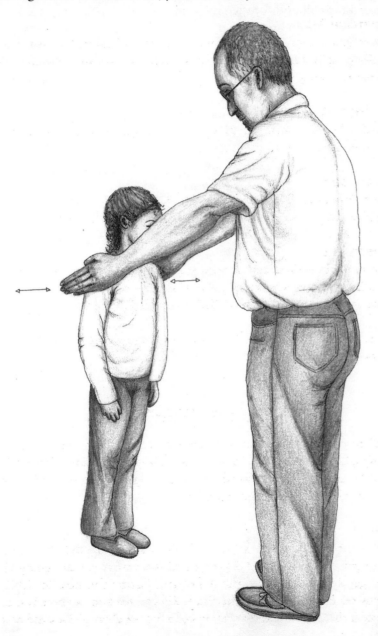

Test 2

Get your child to sit in front of you with arms outstretched and the index finger of each hand pointing directly at your nose. With eyes closed the child must touch their nose and then point at your nose, firstly with the index finger of the right hand and then with the left. This should be repeated several times consecutively and must be done with the eyes closed. Note if one finger repeatedly misses the nose or if there is a slight hesitation before the finger touches the nose. Tick the box for the finger (left or right) that repeatedly misses the target or has a slight tremor before making contact.

Test 3

With your child seated in front of you, have them stretch their arms out in front of them, just like Superman in flight. With their eyes open they then turn their hands to the palms-up position and rapidly alternate the movement: palms-down/palms-up. Look for the hand that goes out of sync first or the elbow that bends and then tick the appropriate box.

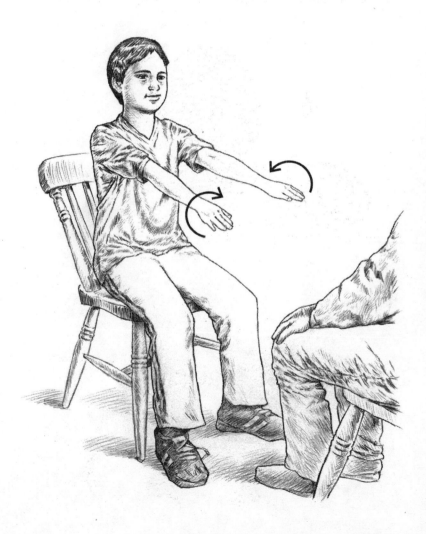

Test 4

With your child sitting facing you, have them place their elbows by their side with forearms outstretched in front of them, palms upwards. They then have to turn their hands palms-down/palms-up as rapidly as possible while keeping their elbows by their side. Note which hand goes out of sync first or which wrist bends producing a waving movement. Tick the box as to which wrist bends – left or right.

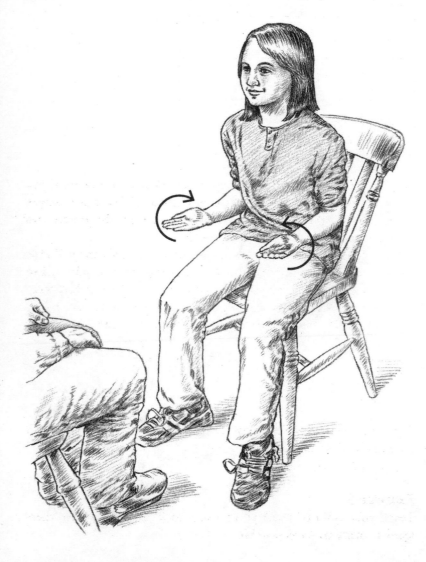

Test box

	RIGHT	LEFT
Test 1		
Test 2		
Test 3		
Test 4		
TOTAL		

Now look at your test box. If three or more ticks are left or right you are safe to proceed with the following exercises. **If you are unsure about any of the results or the results are evenly mixed you should consult an experienced practitioner.**

The following exercises should only be started once the child has completed the general exercises 1 to 3 or, for younger children, 4 to 5 described above. Here we will assume that you have ticked three or four of the **LEFT** boxes. If you have ticked three or four of the **RIGHT** boxes then simply swap right for left in the instructions given below.

Exercise 1

Each day when your child brushes their teeth, have them use their left hand and stand on their left leg.

Exercise 2

Teach your child to use a yo-yo using their left hand. Have them learn as many tricks as possible.

Exercise 3
Younger children can trace mazes using their left hand.

Exercise 4
Get younger children to stand on their left leg, hum a tune and conduct the orchestra using their left hand.

Exercise 5
Younger children, or children that cannot/will not do the exercises described above, can be sat on a chair that rotates and spun *slowly* to the left. After every two or three rotations, say 'boo' to gain the child's attention and look at their eyes. If the eyes are flicking from side to side you have overdone it and will need to reduce the number of times you rotate the chair. You will need to do this spin chair exercise 3 times a day.

If you ticked three or four boxes on the **LEFT** you can also do the following:

- Have your child spend six minutes a day searching for Wally in the *Where's Wally* books
- For older children, have them spend ten minutes a day doing wordsearches (wordsearch books can be purchased at all good bookshops)
- Show your child pictures of unfamiliar faces (you can cut these out of magazines or use Steve McCurry's excellent book, *Portraits*); only allow ten seconds per picture

Once your child has been doing these activities for a couple of weeks you can have them listen to music at the same time. The music should be listened to via the **LEFT** ear only and should *not* be accompanied by any singing. You will need to use an earplug-type earphone to achieve this.

If you ticked off three or four boxes on the **RIGHT** you can also do the following:

- Show your child pictures of familiar faces and ask them to talk about or describe the person (you can cut pictures of pop stars/TV celebrities out of magazines)
- Create a list of fifty words containing five categories of ten words e.g. animals, plants, vegetables, countries, furniture,

etc., then read the words out and have your child write them down in groups according to the category in which they belong

- Have your child stand on their right leg and carry out some mental arithmetic appropriate to their age, e.g. subtracting 7's from 100

Again, once your child has been doing these activities for a couple of weeks you can have them listen to music at the same time. The music should be listened to via the **RIGHT** ear only and *should* be accompanied by singing. You will need to use an earplug-type earphone to achieve this.

The physical exercises should be continued until they are perfected. The other activities can be continued with variations on each theme for four to six weeks. Once a week, retest your child and compare the results with the original tick box. If your child continues to struggle with the exercises or shows no sign of progress after, say, two months, consider contacting a Tinsley House Treatment Centre for advice – at www.tinsleyhouseclinic.com, 'Finding a clinic near you' is on the first page.

The eyes have it – Sam, aged 7 years

Sam came into the world following the perfect pregnancy, a short labour and a trouble-free delivery. He attained the perfect APGAR score, no jaundice was evident and, being the sensible chap that he is, he took to the breast with gusto. All his developmental milestones were achieved on time and when he started preschool he mixed well with other children, shared toys and sat quietly on the mat at story time. In fact, until Year 2 of primary school he was the perfect child in every way.

Now imagine the shock Sam's parents received when they were told at a parents' evening that Sam was falling behind at school and it was suggested he should be tested for dyslexia. The next day Sam's mother was pouring her heart out to her best friend over the phone when her teaching-assistant friend interrupted her and told her about a book that the SENCO (special educational needs co-ordinator) at her school had been talking about – Is That My Child? Three days later the book had been purchased and inwardly digested, the diet put in place and essential fatty-acid supplementation started. Sam started doing the stair exercises described in the book under the watchful eye of his mother and after six weeks could do them perfectly. It was at this point that Sam's mother contacted the clinic and made an appointment for an assessment.

*On talking to Sam's mum it became clear that there was an extended family history of developmental delay on the father's side of the family and that Sam had gradually been showing signs of developmental delay himself. Several early signs of a potentially developing problem had been put down to him 'just being a boy'. He had always been a **messy eater**, could trip over a matchstick and still had **problems in physically dressing himself**. As the schoolwork had gradually become harder he was showing (albeit insidiously) increasing levels of **inattention**, was increasingly **fidgety** and had become a master of diversionary/avoidance tactics. So now not only was there a possibility that Sam might have dyslexia, but it was looking increasingly likely that he also had aspects of **dyspraxia** and **attention deficit**.*

Once I started to examine Sam, a smile must have unknowingly crept across my face, as his mother suddenly interjected with 'What?' Using a standard eye test chart it was evident that Sam had perfect 20/20 vision, but on testing convergence (the ability to bring both eyes in towards the nose accurately) he failed abysmally. Having tested this crudely using an isopter (an inverted cocktail stick) I then tested his convergence/divergence using a computer-generated programme that would give me a printout in diopters, thus providing a much-needed objective measurement of his problem. Put simply, Sam's left eye was slow to move in towards his nose and when it eventually did it could not maintain this new position and flicked back out again.

The rest of the examination confirmed my thoughts that Sam had a significant degree of dyspraxia, secondary dyslexia and consequently a hard time trying to remain focused on something that was far harder to do than it should be. That is, the left side of the cerebellum (back of the brain) together with the right side of the brain were underfunctioning, thus generating the dyspraxia, but this was also causing the left eye to fail in convergence, which was making reading a nightmare. (Try covering your left eye for the next hour and see how you get on. DO NOT try this when you are driving as your ability to judge distances and approach speeds will be seriously impaired.)

Sorting Sam out was a doddle. The logic is, if you can't see close-up you can't read easily, and if you can't read easily you become inattentive and a fidget-bottom. So if you fix the convergence, reading becomes easier, the child can focus and hopefully sit still. Sometimes a little area of the right side of the brain called the anterior cingulate also needs some attention, but in this case Sam never looked back. He used a computer-generated treatment programme daily for a few weeks and before long was reading of his own volition.

Convergence failure has been found to occur in 57 per cent of the children attending the clinic. Therefore, the ability to bring the eyes into convergence should always be tested and secondary dyslexia always considered a possibility.

SO HOW DOES IT WORK?

General exercises – these non-specific exercises are designed to challenge the cerebellum, making the 'weaker' side come up to speed.

LEFT/RIGHT-specific cerebellar exercises are designed to challenge one cerebellar hemisphere via the need to balance and/or produce novel movements

LEFT/RIGHT-specific brain exercises are designed to challenge known functions of the left/right cerebral hemispheres. To give you an example of this, look at the letter T below:

```
         IIIIIIIIIIIIII
         IIIIIIIIIIIIII
              III
              III
              III
              III
              III
```

If you look at the letter 'T' from a distance you are using the right side of the brain. Once you look at the detail and see it is made up from the letter 'I' you are using the left side of the brain. The right side of the brain sees the big picture while the left side examines the detail. There are a great many functions that are specifically left/right and some that can be attributed to specific areas of the brain on one side. By knowing the sidedness of these functions it is possible to 'exercise' set areas of the brain.

The exercises and activities described above are intended to help children with learning/behavioural problems. If you have any concerns about your child's health you should contact a health professional for advice.

5

HOW FOOD AFFECTS THE BRAIN AND BEHAVIOUR

The food your child eats has an immense effect on their brain and behaviour. Good nutrition is needed for the brain's construction, and to keep its development on schedule.

Poor nutrition is holding many children back. It hampers their physical and mental development, and stops them fulfilling their true potential.

WHAT THE BRAIN NEEDS

Amino acids

These are the building blocks of protein. When you eat protein, it is digested and broken down into amino acids, which your body can use to build new proteins. These are used for growth, to produce new cells, and to repair damaged tissues and organs.

In common with the rest of the body, the brain needs amino acids for maintenance and repair. But it also has its own special requirement – for producing neurotransmitters. These are chemical signalling molecules used to transmit messages between cells within the brain, and also between the other cells of the nervous system.

The brain, and the rest of the central nervous system (CNS), is made up of billions of cells called neurons. There are many kinds of neurons – those in the brain are different from those in nerves, for example – but all must be able to communicate with one another, in order for information to be received and comprehended by the brain, decisions to be made, messages transmitted to the rest of the body, and actions (such as moving a finger or turning to look at something) carried out.

Messages are transmitted between neurons by chemical messengers called neurotransmitters. Here's how it happens. The cells in the nervous system aren't physically 'joined' – there are tiny gaps between them, called synapses, and messages between cells have to 'jump' across these gaps. These jumps are performed by neurotransmitters. When a cell releases a neurotransmitter, the neurotransmitter molecules pass across the synapse, and are taken up by special receptors on the cell next door, which then receives the 'message'. This cell, in turn, can pass the message on to cells that it is adjacent to, by releasing its own neurotransmitters for them to receive. In this way, chemical messages are transmitted around the body.

Each time this happens the cell that sent the chemical message is triggered to produce more protein and the cell that received that message has an increased potential to do the same. The more times a cell is brought to threshold (made to pass on the message) the more protein it produces and the healthier it becomes, as these proteins are needed both to keep the cell in good repair and to produce more neurotransmitters. Thus the more your child uses a pathway in their brain – like learning their spellings – the better it works.

But there is more to our brains than just nerve cells. A few years ago another cell type found in the brain was considered to be little more than just bubble wrap holding the brain together. Now we know these astrocytes, as they are called, are as important as neurons and may prove to be even more so. Earlier we mentioned the neuron types specific to the great apes and man, which in the human brain develop some four months after birth. Now new evidence is emerging that our brains also contain astrocytes unique to our species.

FACT

- Did you know that with the right mental exercises your brain can literally grow in size and complexity?
- Did you know that following his death Einstein's brain was removed and is preserved to this day?
- Did you know that Einstein's genius has been attributed to the vast number of astrocytes in his brain?

A steady energy supply

The brain is the most energy-hungry organ in the body. Although it makes up only about 5 per cent of a child's body weight, it uses an amazing 30 per cent of the body's 'fuel requirements' in the form of blood glucose. The brain relies upon a sugar called glucose for its energy supply, and because the brain cannot store glucose, it needs a steady supply.

Modern children's diets, however, are far more likely to provide the brain with 'glucose rushes' separated by 'glucose dips', leading to mood and energy swings, as we shall discover later in this book. These sugar highs and lows not only play havoc with the brain's pleasure centre but leave the pancreas – the organ that produces insulin – not knowing if it is coming or going. And we all know what happens if the pancreas packs up: diabetes.

Healthy fats

An amazing 60 per cent of the brain's dry weight is composed of fat, which is constantly being 'recycled' and replenished. A child's brain needs a supply of fats to keep this continuous process functioning smoothly, but these are not just any old fats. The fats used by the brain are mainly the so-called essential fatty acids, or EFAs.

Unfortunately, the healthy 'brain fats' our children need are all too often crowded out by the 'bad fats' found in junk food.

Water

The brain, like the rest of the body, needs water. Many of the symptoms of dehydration are related to the effect of water deprivation on the brain.

WHAT THE BRAIN DOESN'T NEED

Anti-nutrients

There are several 'anti-nutrients' that interfere with the brain's development and function. Some of these, including stimulants such as caffeine, affect the brain's function directly. Other food compounds compete with the 'proper' nutrients in order to be incorporated into the brain's structure. Unhealthy foods also crowd out more nutritious foods from children's diets, leaving them more at risk of nutritional deficiencies that could harm or hinder their brains' development and function.

If your child does not eat a healthy diet, their brain will not be functioning at its best. Their mood will also suffer. Poor diets, associated with too many unhealthy fats and too much refined sugar, along with deficiencies in essential healthy fats, vitamins and minerals, can play havoc with young people's emotional states.

However, a healthy diet, concentrating on the nutrients that the brain needs most, can:

- 'Improve' behaviour (including reducing aggression)
- Help children to stay calm and focused
- Boost learning ability and intellectual performance
- Improve the ability to concentrate
- Improve memory
- Reduce tiredness

Thought to be autistic – Aiden, aged 3 years

*Apart from his mother's blood pressure rising towards the end of her pregnancy, Aiden's passage into the world would have been perfect were it not for the fact he disgraced himself just before the event by emptying his bowels. The resultant **meconium** can cause problems to the foetus/baby if taken in, but he survived the 'disgrace' to go on to achieve all his milestones until his second year. At that point he developed his own language, became a **toe-walker**, avoided **eye contact**, had periods of **hyperactivity** and would play around children and never with them. He was **clumsy**, would only feed himself with his finger, was **messy** and could not or would not dress himself. Aiden* *could not focus on anything, needed a comforter at all times and would constantly sniff or make animal noises.*

*His medical history contained **eczema, asthma, glue ear** and a very unpleasant-looking contagious skin condition. When he first came to see me he was considered to be within the autistic spectrum.*

Watching Aiden as I talked to his mother my heart was sinking lower and lower. Lastly, we talked about his diet. Aiden had always been a fussy eater and from eighteen months onwards had basically dictated his own diet, spitting out anything that met with his disapproval. Now his self-dictated diet consisted of toast with chocolate spread for breakfast, marmite and cheese sandwiches for lunch with twiglets, and boiled egg or cereal for his evening meal. Snacks were biscuits or crisps and the only thing he would drink was blackcurrant cordial (containing aspartame).

Aiden was, to say the least, somewhat difficult to examine, but we got there eventually and the outcome was no surprise to me. Now came the tricky bit – convincing his mother of the need for change and getting Aiden to be compliant and accept the dietary changes I felt necessary, together with the addition of omega-3 and -6 supplements, vitamins and the daily exercise regime to be carried out at home. Having explained the changes necessary within his diet I then suggested coping strategies his mother could put in place and the parental control methods I was sure she would need, at least during the transition period.

When we next met some six weeks later I could hardly believe my eyes. Aiden was calm, there was no sign of the grubby comforter and he complied with my requests to examine him without the slightest hesitation or protest. As his mother described the changes in him she was close to tears and when she left that day she thanked me for giving her back her son.

From that day on Aiden has not looked back and each visit to the clinic brings news of new achievements and continuing progress.

Labelling and pigeonholing children has certain advantages, particularly if you are considering having your child statemented, but if the label is inaccurate or wrong it can prevent an accurate assessment and thereby effective treatment.

6

NUTRITION AND DEVELOPMENTAL DELAY SYNDROMES

While good nutrition is important for all children, it is crucial for children with any kind of learning or behavioural difficulty.

By emphasising the slow-release carbohydrates, protein, healthy fats and fruit and vegetables recommended in this book, we can provide your child's brain with the nutrients it needs in order to develop and function to its full potential. It *is* possible for children with developmental delay syndromes to 'catch up'. And our healthy diet will support their progress.

An unhealthy diet, full of junk food, unhealthy fats, sugar and salt will hold your child back, by starving their brain of the building blocks it needs, and 'poisoning' it with harmful additives and 'anti-nutrients'.

The tremendous impact of diet on behaviour isn't hard to see. Many parents notice that certain foods – usually sugary and sweetened drinks, sweets and additive-laden sweet snacks – have an almost immediate effect on their child. They say their child becomes 'hyper'. 'Bouncing off the walls' is another phrase we commonly hear.

Parents have also seen remarkable improvements in their children's behaviour, as well as their ability to concentrate at school, after they 'dumped the junk'. This anecdotal evidence has been backed up by several studies, including one by the Institute for Child Health in London, where hyperactive children were put on a 'few foods' diet (low in additives and common food allergens) and an improvement in their behaviour and scores in psychological tests was noted. When the chemical culprits were allowed back in the children's diets, lo and behold, their behaviour worsened again.

Poor nutrition and nutritional deficiencies could also play a role in antisocial behaviour and even crime. A scientific study in 2002 at a young offender institution in Aylesbury showed that when young men there were fed multivitamins, minerals and essential fatty acids, the number of violent offences they committed in the prison fell by 37 per cent, and offences in general fell by 26 per cent. (Those who were given a placebo (dummy pills) rather than 'real' supplements showed no change in behaviour.) Studies on aggressive alcoholics by America's National Institute for Health are producing similar results.

Controlling ADHD – the pharmaceutical solution

Stimulant drugs were first used to control the symptoms of ADHD way back in the 1930s, but the increasing use of drugs such as Ritalin to treat children with behavioural disorders has recently become a topic of much debate.

There is concern that these powerful medications are doled out too easily – between 1999 and 2004 the number of prescriptions for Ritalin and other members of the methylphenidate drug family doubled. Defenders of the increasing number of stimulant prescriptions to children claim that more drugs are prescribed simply because doctors are becoming more skilled at recognising the subtle signs of ADHD. Their opponents counter that ADHD is over-diagnosed, often in children who are simply 'boisterous'. Perhaps, as the figures would suggest, both learning and behavioural problems are indeed on the increase and this should be ringing alarm bells around the world. Also, we have to consider the use of methylphenidate (one of the drugs used to treat ADHD), obtained without a prescription, as a performance enhancer, and the potential dangers this practice exposes the user to.

It's a sad fact that a large proportion of professionals dealing with children with behavioural problems will simply write out a prescription for a stimulant such as Ritalin for a child they diagnose with ADHD, without considering any other, non-pharmaceutical, treatment. I can sympathise with the parents of children with behavioural disorders and to a certain extent understand the thinking behind the prescribing of certain medications. After all, if it is all you have to offer and as a caring physician you want to do something, it's easy to see why so many prescriptions are written – but this is not the answer. Most health professionals would not have a clue as to where the problems lie in the brain, so how can they possibly help?

I recently attended a series of lectures given by a man considered by many to be a leading expert in the field of learning and behavioural problems in children. He stated that dyslexia is basically a problem with the left side of the brain, while ADD, ADHD, OCD and autism were problems originating from the right side of the brain. When I asked if he could tell me where in the right side of the brain these symptoms originated from he was at a loss to answer. If you don't know that ADD/ADHD is due to the under-functioning of an area called the anterior cingulate gyrus and that autistic traits are due to poorly developing von Economo (spindle) cells, then it is, I believe, a very poor reflection of our state of learning when we wield a chemical cosh in the dark.

Over the years, concern has also grown over the efficacy and safety of medications such as Ritalin. A small but significant number of children prescribed these drugs develop side effects including insomnia, obsessive-compulsive behaviour, agitation and depression.

In addition, Ritalin and the other drugs don't work for every child; in many cases they are ineffective or, as I have been told by so many parents, the symptoms have worsened or the child's appetite is so suppressed that their already poor diet is further restricted. And finally, remember that these drugs only *control* the condition and do not cure it. The methods used at Tinsley House Clinic – diet and supplementation combined with brain exercises – address the blocks on the brain's behaviour, as well as stimulating its proper development.

Nutrition is a better way

Firstly, nutrition is safer. Ritalin and other drugs can have side effects, while the good nutrition and supplements we recommend do not. Surely, if given a choice between two available treatments, one with side effects, the other without, the decision is simple?

Also, encouragingly, there is evidence that nutritional therapy may be *more* effective than drugs in controlling ADHD. Exciting new research published in 2006 from the University of South Australia in Adelaide revealed that omega-3 and omega-6 supplements (the kind we recommend) were actually *more* effective in treating ADHD symptoms than the stimulant drugs. In the largest clinic-based study of its kind, 132 children aged 7 to 12 were given supplements combining omega-3 fish oil and omega-6 evening primrose oil. At the end of the 30-week study, 40 to 50 per cent of the children taking the supplements showed a strong improvement in the core ADHD symptoms of inattention and hyperactivity/ impulsivity, compared to children who were given a placebo. By comparing this efficacy with that of Ritalin calculated in another published study, the researchers were able to conclude that the omegas were more effective.

Addressing behavioural and learning problems through nutrition targets the root causes of the symptoms – it provides the brain with the essential-fatty-acid building blocks it needs in order to develop and function correctly. Children with ADHD, dyslexia and autism have been found to be deficient in these fatty acids. Our dietary recommendations also provide a secure, stable source of energy for the brain, to prevent 'hyper' behaviour and mood swings.

We do not claim that food and supplements alone 'cure' ADHD and other developmental delay syndromes, but they certainly play a vital part in treatment. Without the diet, the treatment cannot be effected.

Ritalin – Darren, aged 12 years

*Darren's mother brought him to see me because she was concerned about his continuing problems and long-term medication. He had been born at full term, following an incident-free pregnancy, by natural delivery. However, he had suffered **foetal distress** and required some assistance immediately following birth. He had been late attaining all his **developmental milestones**, his first words not appearing until two years of age, only to then cease completely, requiring the intervention of a speech therapist. He was dry by day at three and a half years and, unusually, dry by night as well before his third birthday.*

*At playgroup, as elsewhere, he was overly friendly and **very active**. Once in reception he was fidgety, would walk around the classroom doing his own thing, had the **attention span** of a gnat and was overtly **clumsy**. By five years of age he was put on **medication**, which he has had to take ever since, as his mother stated that without it he was hyperactive and **unmanageable**.*

*His medical history included numerous **ear infections** when he was younger. However, on direct questioning, Darren informed me that he suffered frequent headaches over the eyes, had **ringing in the ears** and **blurred vision** when attempting to read.*

His mother had put him on omega-3 a year ago but when she described his diet I came to realise why the omega-3 wasn't helping and why continued medication was necessary. His diet did not contain any fruit whatsoever, just two vegetables that would be eaten occasionally and only modest amounts of protein. Generally, breakfast, snacks, lunch if it occurred, and his evening meal were carbohydrate-laden and drinks were laced with aspartame.

At that first visit I provided Darren and his mother with a dietary plan and some very simple physical exercises to be completed at home on a daily basis. I saw Darren some two months later, when his mother informed me that the first week on the diet was a 'nightmare'. However, the following week his behaviour changed and the school phoned to say they had noticed such a change in him, particularly that now they could reason with him; he was calmer and seemed happier. Two months into the diet and at the next visit his mother informed me that she had taken him off the Ritalin. Darren has some way to go, but already he is functioning at a higher level and he now can feel the difference.

If your child has been prescribed medication you should discuss its withdrawal with the practitioner that prescribed it. Some medications should not be stopped abruptly.

Equasym – Mickey, aged 8 years

*Mickey's passage into the world was not an easy one. After a perfect pregnancy and relatively short labour he went into foetal distress and required a **ventouse**-assisted delivery. He then required suction and a little assistance before he was breathing normally and could be given back to his mother.*

*Apart from sitting unaided, all his developmental milestones were delayed. He was a **bottom-shuffler** and **struggled with his speech**. At nursery school **he kept away from other children and reacted badly to loud or sudden noises**. At school he **struggled with his reading, spellings, maths and handwriting**. He was **clumsy**, had **poor spatial awareness**, was a **messy eater** and was* always the last child to get dressed after sports. Mickey would constantly **fidget**, could not **concentrate** and had a **poor short-term memory.**

His medical history was punctuated with endless **ear infections** and **accidents,** and he had undergone surgery on four occasions to have **grommets** fitted in his ears. He had been prescribed Equasym (methylphenidate hydrochloride, the same active ingredient as Ritalin and Concerta) by his paediatrician.

When I questioned his mother about his **diet** an all too familiar pattern appeared. Every meal was predominately processed carbohydrates, there was no fruit and the only vegetables were hidden in pasta sauces, and even these were out of a jar. Apart from milk with his breakfast the only thing he would drink was fizz out of a can.

Following a detailed examination I talked over the much-needed changes to the diet with Mickey and his mother. I also suggested putting him on a double dose of omega-3 for three months followed by a single dose thereafter. At that point his mother said that she had tried omega-3 in the past but it made him worse. I asked her which brand she had given him and when she told me I knew why it had not worked. Unfortunately, some of the omega-3 and -6 supplements targeted at children contain artificial sweeteners and the brand she had used contained **aspartame**. The last thing on earth a brain that is struggling requires is aspartame or bad E numbers, yet the manufacturers just haven't got the message. Once Mickey and his mother had agreed to try the new diet and proper omega-3 and -6 it was only a matter of adding a few simple exercises to do at home.

Two months later the diet was in place and the supplementation with omega-3 and -6 was taking place on a daily basis with no ill effects as had happened before. One month later, when Mickey was seen again, his mother told me he had a confession to make. He told me he had forgotten to take his medication for a week.

'And?' I said.

'I feel brilliant,' he replied.

Mickey has now started the second phase of his treatment and is using a computer-generated programme at home on a daily basis to improve movements of his left eye in close vision. We have got a few months to go before his schoolwork improves but already he is calmer, can sit still and can focus on the job in hand.

If you decide to supplement your child's diet with omega-3 and omega-6, do check carefully that they do not contain artificial sweeteners or bad E numbers.

Good nutrition can help every child's behaviour

Put simply, here's what you need to do:

- Remove 'junk food'
- Drastically cut down on refined sugars
- Cut out harmful additives wherever possible
- Add good, home-cooked foods
- Add supplements where necessary
- Become an expert at reading food labels

CAN DIET IMPROVE ACADEMIC PERFORMANCE?

If your child's ability to learn is being held back because their diet isn't all it should be, the answer is a resounding yes! Address the nutritional deficiency with good, wholesome food, and supplements where necessary, remove the harmful additives and unhealthy foods, and the block to their progress will be removed. If you take a poorly nourished child and feed them a healthy diet, their school performance will almost certainly improve.

Many nutrient deficiencies, particularly in their early stages, manifest themselves in symptoms such as fatigue, feeling listless and 'out of sorts', and psychological problems such as depression. This is certainly true in the case of vitamin C deficiency (well before you see the symptoms of full-blown scurvy). And iron-deficiency anaemia leads to fatigue, tiredness and difficulty in concentration. Any of these symptoms will make it difficult for a child to study.

Tiredness in class can also be a result of low blood sugar, which can occur if children skip breakfast. A huge volume of

---

research has shown that children eating a healthy breakfast perform better at school, and we'll be exploring the fascinating importance of the first meal of the day later in this book.

A child who is acting up and talking back to their teacher, will also not be learning much. And once again, there is evidence for a healthy diet and appropriate supplements improving children's behaviour.

7

BASIC NUTRITION FOR CHILDREN

What are today's children eating? The most recent official National Diet and Nutrition Survey for children makes depressing reading – the foods most commonly eaten are white bread, crisps, biscuits, potatoes and chocolate. By contrast, children aren't eating enough fruit and vegetables – only 10 per cent reach their target of 'five-a-day'. Other findings include:

- 53 per cent of children surveyed did not eat raw vegetables or salad
- 40 per cent did not eat cooked vegetables
- 60 per cent did not eat cooked green leafy vegetables
- 11 per cent of boys and 7 per cent of girls ate *no* fruit or vegetables
- 75 per cent of children drank fizzy drinks

Fatter, and poorly nourished

The National Diet and Nutrition Survey found that children's average calorie intakes were lower than the estimated average requirement, and lower than previous generations. Yet still the problem of childhood obesity is burgeoning, so what's going on?

It's likely that the main problem is that children today simply don't do as much as when the official calorie requirements were set. Today's youngsters need to be much more active. Even though they're eating less than their parents did when they were younger, their exercise and physical activity just isn't enough to burn up the food they are eating.

Not only are today's children eating fewer calories than previously, the make-up of their diets is more likely to be skewed in favour of unhealthy saturated and trans (hydrogenated) fats, sugar and salt. For instance:

- They're consuming over one-and-a-half times more sugar than they should be – most of this coming from fizzy drinks
- The proportion of saturated fat in children's diets is nearly one-and-a-half times higher than it should be

Children are also more likely to be deficient in nutrients, because they're eating more nutritionally poor processed foods, and less of the wholefoods such as pulses, lean meat and fish, wholegrain carbohydrates, and fresh fruit and vegetables – the sort of food their young bodies are crying out for. A worryingly high proportion of children don't get enough vitamin A (vital for healthy skin and eyes) and zinc (which is crucial for brain function, as well as for the immune system).

WHAT BRITAIN'S TEENAGERS ARE EATING

Another recent national diet survey revealed that British teenagers ate more fast food, sweets and chocolates – foods generally high in fat, especially harmful saturated and trans fats, sugar and salt – than any other age group. They were also deficient in fibre and several other important minerals and vitamins.

Teenage diets are generally lacking in fruit and vegetables – the very foods that could help to displace junk foods and help weight control, as well as being packed with antioxidants and fibre.

WHY DO TEENAGERS EAT SO BADLY?

Hormones have a lot to answer for, but they can't take all the blame.

In the past scientists believed that brain development stopped in early childhood, but new research has found that it continues into the twenties. One of the important parts of the brain involved in this adolescent rewiring is the one responsible for decision-making and risk-taking. This accounts for much of the teenage bravado and the belief that nothing can harm them. They feel invincible. It also helps to explain why so many of the health messages targeted at adolescents fail miserably – teenagers just don't see what they consider 'old people's diseases' as a threat to them.

You can actually directly relate the level of a substance called monoamine oxidase (MAO) to the level of risk a person is likely to take. The higher the level of MAO, the more likely you are not only to engage in dangerous activities, but also to fail to see the danger. And guess who has the highest naturally occurring levels of MAO? Teenagers in general, and boys in particular.

It's hardly surprising that we are seeing an 'epidemic' of obesity, the first signs of 'adult-onset' diseases such as atherosclerosis (clogged arteries), high blood pressure, and diabetes in children, not to mention the rise in 'psychological' problems among youngsters, many of which are caused or exacerbated by poor diets. And even if they feel fine now, these children are storing up health problems for the future.

CHOLESTEROL AND AGGRESSION

High levels of cholesterol in the blood have been associated with an increased risk of heart disease, but did you know that *low* levels have been linked to an increased risk of violent death due to either accidents or suicide?

Experiments, albeit in monkeys, have found that our furry friends become distinctly more aggressive if fed on a low-cholesterol diet. Coupled with this it has been found that these very touchy primates also have reduced levels of certain breakdown products of metabolism, suggesting a low level of a very important substance called serotonin. Now the plot thickens, for it has been found that low levels of serotonin are associated with increased levels of food-seeking and risk-taking.

Cholesterol is needed for many important functions of the body including the production of the cell walls of nerves, and typically is found in foods that are energy rich. As our predecessors could not pop down to the local supermarket and stock up the larder in the way we can now, they had to rely upon the somewhat precarious and unpredictable process of hunting. In this situation, when perhaps you haven't eaten for a few days, it might prove to be a good move if a member of the hunting party showed exceptional valour (or reckless stupidity) in the hope that everyone would have juicy mammoth steaks for tea.

Thus the cholesterol/serotonin balance may have been a great advantage to our distant relatives, giving them an extra edge while hunting and a reward if successful. This basic drive is rarely needed in a modern complex industrialised society but it may go a long way to explain the urge many people feel to eat calorific energy and cholesterol-rich foods.

Children and choice

Today's young people have far more choice over what they eat than previous generations. They have more say over what the family eats, and also eat more outside the home.

Study after study has shown that, in general, the more choice children have over their food, the less healthy their diets will be. Given the choice, they will choose cola over water or fruit juice to drink, fried nuggets over grilled chicken for lunch, and chocolate biscuits and sweets over fruit or vegetable sticks for a snack.

The problem is, if you come down too hard, and your child thinks you are cutting all the nice things out of their diet, they will rebel – and eat as much of the unhealthy foods as they can when you're not around. You need to give them some choice, but within your own healthy limits.

Persuading children

It's not that children don't know which foods are healthy and which aren't, it's just that the reasons we give for avoiding the 'junk' aren't convincing enough to young minds. When it tastes good, and all your friends are eating it, being told 'It's not good for you' doesn't cut much ice. Warnings about 'adult' diseases like heart disease, type-2 diabetes, cancer and stroke don't work – when you're a child, all those kinds of thing only happen to 'old people'.

A better way to get children on board is to set a good example (why should you expect them to eat healthily if you live on pizza?), and use arguments that show what's in it for them. Tell your children that healthy food will help them to concentrate and do better in school, to run faster in the playground, and give them clearer skin and shinier hair. Once they begin to feel the benefits of good food over junk, in terms of better concentration, energy levels and all-round health, it's much easier to keep them on the nutritional straight and narrow. Better still, put them on a healthy diet from day one – breast is best if at all possible, followed by a junk-free healthy diet.

And as they will know no different, the chances are they too will provide a healthy diet for their children. I see a lot of overweight children in the company of overweight parents and when I suggest the whole family should embrace healthy eating then, strangely enough, as the child loses weight so do the parents. So much for the genetics excuse.

WHAT DO CHILDREN NEED TO EAT?

Children, like the rest of us, need a balanced diet. They need protein, carbohydrates and healthy fats, along with vitamins and minerals. Water and fibre are essential, too.

Because children are growing and developing, their needs for certain nutrients are higher. They also need proportionally more calories than adults – as growing takes a lot of energy.

But although growing bodies need more calories to sustain them, you need to be careful that intakes of fat (especially saturated fat) and sugar don't outstrip them!

Age	5–6		7–10		11–14		15–18	
	Boys	Girls	Boys	Girls	Boys	Girls	Boys	Girls
Calorie requirement	1,715	1,545	1,970	1,740	2,220	1,845	2,755	2,100

Remember, these recommendations are for an 'average' child – and we all know there's no such thing as 'average' when it comes to children!

Protein

Children need protein for body growth and repair. Protein building blocks called amino acids are used to build new cells and tissues, and repair those that wear out. As we mentioned earlier, not only are amino acids used to build tissues like bone, muscle and blood cells, they are also needed to produce the body's chemical messengers – hormones that are carried around the bloodstream, and the neurotransmitters that transmit messages in the brain and nervous system.

Children need a relatively large protein intake for their size, but fortunately this is easy to achieve, and protein deficiency is extremely rare in the developed world.

More of a problem is the *quality* of protein in children's diets. You need to ensure that your child's protein comes from sources that are low in unhealthy fats, salt and additives.

Good protein sources for children:

- Lean meat
- Poultry
- Fish
- Eggs
- Low-fat dairy foods (milk, yoghurt, cheese)
- Pulses (beans and lentils)
- Nuts and seeds

Watch out for processed protein! It's generally much higher in fat, salt, additives and even sugar. Processed meat and poultry products are generally high in fat, and many contain a lot of added bulkers and fillers, water, salt and other preservatives. So try to avoid:

- Burgers
- Chicken nuggets
- Sausages
- Re-formed chicken and fish 'shapes' for children
- Re-formed sliced meat and poultry

All of the list above are likely to be low in 'real' meat, and high in other nasties. Some responsible manufacturers make sausages, burgers, nuggets, etc. with a high meat content, but you really do need to do your detective work and study the label (see Chapter 9).

You can also make low-fat versions of your children's fast-food favourites, such as burgers and chicken nuggets – you'll find some recipes in this book.

Animal versus vegetable

Animal protein sources, like meat, poultry, fish and dairy products, are easier for the body to use and absorb than vegetarian protein from beans, nuts, seeds and the like. But on the flip side, animal protein is also much higher in saturated fat (more about this unhealthy fat later).

It is generally best for children to get their protein from as wide a variety of sources as possible.

You can minimise the saturated fat in your protein foods by:

- Avoiding 'processed protein' (see the list above)
- Trimming the fat from meat
- Buying lean meat and mincing it yourself – bought mince often has a lot of fat minced in
- Removing the skin from chicken – this is where you'll find most of the fat
- Choosing low-fat dairy products such as semi-skimmed or skimmed milk, low-fat yoghurt, low-fat spreads and low-fat cheese

Carbohydrates

Carbohydrates are the body's main and most easily available energy source. Children need sufficient carbohydrates to fuel their growing bodies, but many children get most of their carbohydrates from unhealthy sources such as sugary foods. This contributes to a whole host of problems, from up-and-down energy levels and hyperactivity, to tooth decay, obesity and therefore a predisposition to high blood pressure, heart disease and cancer.

The best sources of carbohydrates for children are starchy carbohydrates, such as bread, rice, pasta and porridge – but in moderation. Toast for breakfast, pizza for lunch and pasta every evening constitutes carbohydrate abuse! The wholegrain versions (wholemeal bread, rice, brown pasta) are the best carbohydrates of all.

When 'brown' foods are refined into white, much of their nutrient content, as well as their fibre, is stripped away. Wholegrains are also better at balancing children's energy and blood-sugar levels, which we shall explain in more detail later.

The least healthy sources of carbohydrates for children are refined sugars, such as those found in sweets, chocolate, breakfast cereals, ice cream, cakes, biscuits and other sweet snacks, as well as the table sugar your child might sprinkle on cereal or strawberries.

Refined sugars can do dreadful things to your children's blood-sugar levels, and therefore their energy levels and concentration (see Chapter 9). In addition, sugary foods often provide 'empty calories'. In other words, aside from the energy (calories) they contain, there are very few nutrients to speak of. For example, consider a can of cola and the sugar it contains. Aside from water and calories, that can's nutritional content is a big, fat zero, and the only other ingredients are likely to be flavourings and other additives.

And although biscuits, pastries, ice cream, cakes and chocolate contain other ingredients apart from sugar (so they're not so 'empty' in nutritional terms as pure sugar and sweets), they're often high in saturated fat and additives, which are definitely not the kind of thing you want your child to be eating.

Fibre

Many children, especially those with Developmental Delay Syndrome, suffer from poor digestion.

A child's digestive system needs:

- Well-chewed, nutritious food
- Something to work on – fibre
- A healthy balance of bacteria in the gut

There are two kinds of fibre – insoluble and soluble.

Insoluble fibre

This is the kind we used to call 'roughage', but it would really be better to call it 'smoothage', as it smoothes food through the digestive system. Because the body can't digest insoluble fibre, it bulks up the food in children's digestive systems, giving the intestines something to 'work on', and helps prevent diarrhoea and constipation.

Good sources of insoluble fibre include:

- Wholegrains – e.g. wholemeal bread, brown pasta, brown rice, oats, wholegrain breakfast cereals (including muesli) barley, buckwheat
- Vegetables and fruit (especially the skins)

Soluble fibre

This is a 'sticky' kind of fibre that can help lower cholesterol levels. It also keeps children feeling full between meals, and helps prevent their blood-sugar levels from rising too rapidly.

Good sources of soluble fibre include:

- Oats
- Fruit (especially apples)
- Peas, beans and lentils

Soluble fibre not only benefits the heart by helping to control cholesterol levels, it's good for the gut as well.

Although people can't digest soluble fibre, the friendly bacteria in the bowel can. And these beneficial bugs produce chemicals called short-chain fatty acids, which nourish and protect the cells lining the intestinal wall. Numerous books and articles have been written about this subject relating the 'Leaky Gut Syndrome' to autism. If you get the diet right you are taking a huge step in the right direction.

> ## EAT PLANTS FOR FIBRE
>
> The best way to incorporate fibre into your child's diet is to give them plenty of foods that come from plants – wholegrains, fruit and vegetables.
>
> But go slowly if your child isn't used to eating high-fibre foods – not only are they likely to rebel if suddenly all their food is 'brown', a sudden increase in fibre could make them feel uncomfortable and bloated, until their digestive system gets used to it.

Friendly bacteria

You've probably heard of 'friendly bacteria', the so-called 'beneficial gut flora' that help keep us healthy.

There are hundreds of species of bacteria that should be living in your child's digestive system, and most of these are protective. It's a competitive world in a child's gut, with a battle going on between the beneficial bacteria and the less-friendly bugs that could make a child ill. By ensuring your child has a flourishing population of 'good' bacteria, the harmful germs are crowded out.

There are two ways of tipping the balance in favour of the friendly bacteria, thus preventing the harmful bugs from gaining the upper hand. You may have seen products in the supermarket labelled probiotics and prebiotics – these both aim to boost the friendly bacteria, but in different ways.

Probiotics

Probiotic products contain actual cultures of live friendly bacteria, to supplement those living in your child's digestive system. But the bacteria face a difficult journey to reach the intestines, which is to be their final destination and new home. On the way, they have to pass through the stomach, where conditions are extremely acidic, and some studies suggest that most of the bacteria are killed before reaching and setting up home in the bowel.

If your child has a healthy digestive system already, you probably won't see any improvement with probiotics – they seem to produce the best effects in people with 'troublesome tummies' and conditions such as irritable bowel syndrome (IBS), which is rare in children. But there's another kind of 'bacteria booster', which might have more potential for keeping children's friendly bacteria flourishing.

Prebiotics

Prebiotics aren't bacteria, they're bacteria food. These compounds can't be digested by humans, so they pass through our stomach and digestive system until they reach the bowel, where they provide a good meal for the friendly bacteria. The harmful bacteria, however, can't eat prebiotics, so the beneficial bugs get a good meal and flourish, while the bad bacteria go hungry.

And the advantage that prebiotics have over probiotics is, because they're not alive, they can't be killed by the acid conditions of the stomach.

You can buy probiotics and prebiotics in capsules and powder form. They're also added to a variety of products, including yoghurts, drinks and breakfast cereals, but these are generally very high in sugar, so capsules and powders are probably best if you're trying to cut down your child's refined-sugar intake, as this book recommends.

TIPS FOR A HAPPY DIGESTIVE SYSTEM

- Keep your child's fibre intake up, with plenty of wholegrains, pulses (beans and lentils), fruit and vegetables.
- Make sure your child drinks enough – preferably pure water. But don't give them too much at or just before mealtimes – it will fill them up too much, and they'll lose their appetite for the food you've prepared.
- Ban fizzy drinks.
- Make sure your child eats sitting at the table, preferably with the family, rather than walking around, on a tray on their lap watching the television or lying on the floor.
- Encourage your child to chew their food well – good digestion begins in the mouth.

> - Although conversation during family mealtimes is to be encouraged, children still need to concentrate on their food. So don't let your child watch TV, read books at the table, or eat their meals while they're working or playing on their computer.
> - Consider giving your child one of the many probiotic and prebiotic supplements available.

Fats

Too much fat is bad for children – it can cause them to become overweight or obese, which is bad for anyone's health.

But everyone – and especially children – needs a certain amount of fat in order to remain healthy. And some kinds of fat are positively healthy.

We need fat:

- For energy – fat can be broken down to provide fuel for the body
- To protect our organs such as the kidneys and liver (though only a thin layer is necessary – too much fatty padding is unhealthy)
- To build cell membranes
- For healthy brain function
- For the fat-soluble vitamins: vitamins A, D, E and K
- To maintain the oil content of the skin and hair – a diet too low in fat can lead to flaky skin and dry hair
- To produce essential hormones

Once again, the *kind* of fat is important. Saturated fats are harmful to health, so you should minimise them in your child's diet. 'Trans' fats, found in hydrogenated or partially hydrogenated fats, are even worse. But the unsaturated fats (the so-called monounsaturates and polyunsaturates, which include the omega-3 and omega-6 essential fatty acids) are very healthy. The 'omegas' are crucial in brain function, a subject we shall investigate in much more detail later in this book (see Chapter 11).

Unhealthy fats

These are generally solid at room temperature, and include:

- Saturated fats: found in animal products – meat (especially processed meats), dairy products and eggs
- Trans (partially hydrogenated) fats: found in processed foods, and used for frying in many fast-food restaurants

Healthy fats

These are generally liquid at room temperature (they are oils), and include:

- Monounsaturated fats: found in vegetable oils, such as olive, canola, peanut and sesame oil, as well as the oil found in avocados – the oils found in nuts and seeds are also a good source of monounsaturates
- Polyunsaturated fats: found in vegetable oils such as sunflower, safflower and corn oils – the oils found in oily fish (such as salmon, sardines, mackerel and fresh tuna) are rich in a kind of polyunsaturated fat called omega-3 fatty acids, which are particularly important for the brain

Water

Our bodies are composed of approximately 65 per cent water, and a loss of just 1 or 2 per cent can leave us feeling fuzzy-headed. Any further loss leads to symptoms of headaches, impaired concentration, slowed reaction time, irritability, lethargy and tiredness. A loss of more than 8 per cent or so of your bodyweight is life-threatening.

Children become dehydrated more rapidly than adults, and they are also less sensitive to thirst, so they leave it for longer before fetching or asking for a drink.

No one – especially a child – should wait until they're thirsty before drinking. By the time you're thirsty, you're on the way to dehydration. Adults need approximately 1.5 to 2 litres of water a day, which amounts to about 8 to 10 tall glasses. Children need around 8 to 10 *small* glasses.

Encourage your child to regularly top up their fluid levels with healthy drinks.

Drinks for children – what you need to know

The two best drinks for children are water and milk (skimmed or semi-skimmed). Water is best for hydration, and milk, while less hydrating, is highly nutritious.

The problem is, many children would prefer to drink highly sweetened fizzy drinks and squashes, rather than healthier options. They love them, glugging them back like there's no tomorrow! And once children get used to sweet drinks, that's what they expect – and want – drinks to taste like. Anything else tastes bland.

And there's nothing like sweetened drinks to sharpen a child's sweet tooth, making even naturally sweet foods – like a juicy apple – taste sharp.

But if your child is a bit of a sugar-monkey where drinks are concerned, don't panic! It *is* possible to re-train their taste-buds, so that eventually even the sweetest-toothed child can drink water and enjoy it:

- Make fizzy drinks and squashes a very occasional treat, then phase them out entirely
- Serve pure fruit juice in small glasses and with a meal – at other times, water it down
- Gradually reduce the proportion of juice in the drink
- If your child is a squash-drinker, gradually make it weaker and weaker until they drink pure water

Plain, still water

The ultimate hydrator.

Sparkling, fizzy water

The 'fizz' makes it acidic, so it can erode teeth. And it's not so easy to drink enough, because the bubbles can make children feel full and bloated.

Tea

Tea is not particularly popular with most children, but if your child likes it, don't make it too strong, as the tannin in tea can hinder the uptake of vital minerals, and the caffeine in tea is a stimulant.

Herbal and fruit teas

These are a great healthy choice, as they're free from sugar and additives. Herbal teas are a taste most people don't acquire until they are adults (though if your child likes them, that's fantastic), but fruit teas are a different matter, as they have a sweeter, fruitier taste, which many children enjoy. They can also be served hot or cold.

Milk

Highly nutritious, but less hydrating than pure water – with all those nutrients, you can't fit so much water in. It contains valuable protein, vitamins and minerals, including bone- and tooth-friendly calcium. Semi-skimmed milk is generally best for children, unless you have been advised (by your doctor or a dietician or registered nutritionist) that cutting their fat intake by switching to skimmed milk would be better.

Beware of milkshakes and flavoured milks, which can be packed full of sugar, sweeteners and artificial colourings.

Pure fruit juice

Sweet-tasting, so most children love it, and contains vitamins, antioxidants and phytochemicals (beneficial plant chemicals). One 150ml glass of fruit juice counts towards your child's 'five a day' fruit and vegetable target. But fruit juice is also high in sugars (albeit natural ones) and is acidic, so it can damage children's teeth.

Always check the label when buying fruit juice – you want 100 per cent pure and no added sugar.

Diluted fruit juice

By diluting fruit juice, you can give your children the sweet, fruity taste (and the vitamins), while reducing the acidity of the drink. If they're used to pure juice, decrease the strength gradually – if you dive straight in at 'half and half' dilution, or less, the reaction will almost certainly be 'yuk!'

Vegetable juice

Vegetable juices are great – they taste sweet (particularly carrot and beetroot) but they contain less sugar than pure fruit juices. You can make your own using a juicer, but this can be a big hassle if you're not really into juicing! Fortunately you can buy carrot, beetroot, tomato and mixed-vegetable juices at the supermarket and from health-food stores.

Fruit juice drinks
Don't be misled into thinking that this is the same as pure juice – if you buy 'fruit juice drink' it can contain as little as 5 per cent real juice, and can be full of sugar and sweeteners. With only a very few exceptions, 'fruit juice drink' is basically squash!

Squash
In their favour, squashes can encourage children who are reluctant to drink water to maintain their fluid levels. But squash is acidic, generally high in sugar, and often contains artificial colourings and other additives. Some contain fruit juice, but even 'high juice' squashes generally contain high amounts of sugar as well.

Some squashes are labelled 'no added sugar' or 'sugar free', but this almost certainly means they contain artificial sweeteners instead, and as aspartame has had such a bad press and been associated with 'glutamate storms' (see later in this book) it should not form any part of a child's dietary intake.

If your child doesn't like pure water, and likes a fruity taste, it's far better to give them diluted fruit juice.

Fizzy drinks
We already know children in the UK eat too much sugar – and research shows the main source of this is fizzy drinks. Just one can of cola can contain nearly ten teaspoons of added sugar.

As well as contributing 'invisible' sugar, like all 'sparkling' drinks, fizzy drinks are acidic, so can harm children's teeth.

Are diet drinks any better? Well, they're lower in calories and sugar-free, but they're basically water with added chemicals – artificial sweeteners, flavourings, colourings and the like. In other words, not what our children should be drinking.

Flavoured water
These may sound nice and healthy, but the problem lies in the sugar and/or chemicals that flavour the water. One small point in their favour is the fact that these drinks can encourage children who dislike

water to drink and stay hydrated – but they'd be so much better off with pure water.

Smoothies

Most children love smoothies, which can be a good way of getting vitamins and minerals inside them. They generally contain slightly more fibre than pure juice (though not nearly as much as if your child ate the whole fruit).

Smoothies with milk or yoghurt also contribute valuable nutrients such as protein, calcium and vitamins A, D and E. But because they're so thick and concentrated, they're much less hydrating than water – they're more of a snack than a drink.

How much do smoothies count towards your child's five-a-day fruit and vegetable target? The jury is out on that one. You're only allowed to count one glass of fruit juice, no matter how many you drink. But smoothies can contain some 'bits' as well. Some experts say this means that more than one smoothie can count towards that five-a-day. But surely it's better to err on the side of generosity, and allow one portion from juice *or* smoothies, and get the rest from 'whole' fruit and vegetables.

TIPS TO PERSUADE CHILDREN TO DRINK WATER

- Put a glass of water beside their plate at every meal – don't wait for them to ask for a drink
- Buy a novelty water bottle or a 'squeezy' bottle
- Let them drink through a straw
- Draw funny faces or write messages on their glass using a washable felt tip
- Add a couple of ice cubes – some children prefer really cold water
- Freeze a berry in the centre of ice cubes and add them to their glass of water
- Hang a couple of orange slices on the edge of their glass – they'll also get some extra Vitamin C when they eat the fruit
- Set a good example – make sure the children see you drinking water

---

> ## BEWARE CAFFEINE
>
> Many children (and adults, for that matter) are especially sensitive to the stimulant effects of caffeine – it can make them anxious and agitated, and disrupt their concentration. For more on caffeine, see Chapter 12.

Vitamins and minerals

Vitamins and minerals are called micronutrients, because unlike protein, fats, carbohydrates and water, we only need them in minute amounts – quantities measured in thousandths or hundreds-of-thousandths of a gram per day.

But micronutrients are vital. Many of them act as tiny spark plugs, setting off chemical reactions essential to our body's functioning. Some vitamins are involved in metabolising food, converting carbohydrates, fats and sometimes protein into energy that the body can use. Others help to regulate vital body processes. Vitamins and minerals are also involved in the body's defence, supporting the immune system and protecting the body from attack by harmful substances and germs. And without structural micronutrients, including many of the minerals, our bodies would literally fall to pieces.

Vitamins

We can divide vitamins into two kinds:

- Fat-soluble vitamins – vitamins A, D, E and K
- Water-soluble vitamins – the B-vitamins and vitamin C

Fat-soluble vitamins are stored in our body fat, so we can build up reserves of them, which our bodies tap into on days when we haven't eaten enough of a particular vitamin. This is a very useful system, except when we eat too many of a fat-soluble vitamin, and it accumulates to dangerous levels. In practice, however, this rarely happens, except when people take high doses of vitamins over a long time, or regularly eat too much of very rich sources of fat-soluble vitamins (such as liver, which is very rich in vitamin A). You do need to be more careful where children are concerned, however, because of their smaller body size.

Because they dissolve in water, we lose water-soluble vitamins every time we go to the loo. Because we don't store these vitamins – any excess is flushed out of our bodies – we need to top them up every day.

Fat-soluble vitamins
Vitamin A:

- Keeps skin smooth and supple, as well as maintaining the mucous membranes (the 'skin' lining the 'inside' parts of the body, such as the mouth, eyelids, throat and digestive tract)
- Is essential for vision, especially night vision
- Good animal sources – liver, meat, oily fish, dairy products, eggs
- Good non-animal sources – green vegetables (e.g. spinach, cabbage, broccoli), yellow and orange fruit and vegetables (e.g. apricots, peaches, cantaloupe melon, carrots, sweet potatoes)

Vitamin D:

- Vital for the absorption of calcium, which is needed to build healthy bones and teeth
- Good animal sources – oily fish (e.g. salmon, sardines, mackerel), meat, eggs, dairy products
- Good non-animal sources – a chemical reaction caused by the action of sunlight on the skin enables the body to make and store vitamin D, and about fifteen minutes a day during the summer is enough for most people. Vitamin D is also added to margarines and low-fat spreads, and fortified breakfast cereals

Vitamin E:

- Needed for a healthy reproductive system, as well as supporting our immune system – it's also important for nerves and muscles
- Good non-animal sources – nuts and seeds and their oils, wholemeal bread, wheatgerm, avocado, spinach, broccoli

Vitamin K:

- Needed to enable our blood to clot when we're injured, and for healthy bones
- Good animal sources – eggs, fish oils, dairy products
- Good non-animal sources – green leafy vegetables, also produced in small amounts by harmless bacteria in the gut

Water-soluble vitamins
Vitamin B1 (thiamin):

- Needed to release energy from food
- Good animal sources – liver, lean pork
- Good non-animal sources – unrefined cereals and grains, nuts, seeds, fortified flour

Vitamin B2 (riboflavin):

- Needed to digest and metabolise proteins and carbohydrates. Deficiencies may make you more prone to the effects of stress
- Good animal sources – meat (especially liver), eggs, dairy products
- Good non-animal sources – wholegrains, fortified flour, dark green leafy vegetables such as watercress and spinach

Vitamin B3 (niacin):

- Needed to metabolise our food, and is also involved in the production of hormones
- Good animal sources – meat, dairy products
- Good non-animal sources – fortified flour

Vitamins B1, B2 and B3 are so important that white flour in the UK has to be fortified with them by law (wholemeal flour is already a good source).

Vitamin B6:

- Useful in our metabolism, vitamin B6 may also help to regulate our moods
- Good animal sources – liver, pork, lamb, chicken, eggs, dairy products
- Good non-animal sources – beans (especially soya beans), potatoes, brown rice, wholegrains, wheatgerm, nuts, dark green leafy vegetables

Folic acid:

- Also known as folate, folic acid helps the body to absorb nutrients effectively, and supports the immune system
- During pregnancy, it helps prevent neural tube defects in the developing baby
- Helps prevent a kind of anaemia
- Good animal sources – liver, eggs
- Good non-animal sources – green leafy vegetables, fortified breakfast cereals, pulses (beans and lentils), nuts, citrus fruit, apricots, broccoli, brown rice, wheatgerm

Vitamin B12:

- Needed for the production of red blood cells
- Good animal sources – red meat, fish, shellfish, eggs, dairy products
- Good non-animal sources – not found in vegan foods, but produced in small amounts by harmless bacteria in our guts

Vitamin C:

- Keeps the immune system strong, and is needed for blood clotting and wound healing
- Boosts the body's absorption of iron from food
- Good non-animal sources – fruit (especially kiwi fruit, blackcurrants, strawberries, citrus fruits), yellow and red peppers, tomatoes, Brussels sprouts

Minerals

Certain minerals are essential for our bodies to function properly. Some contribute to our body's structure – for example, about 1.5kg (3lb) of an adult's body weight is the mineral calcium, almost all of it in bones and teeth. Others, like potassium, are involved in maintaining the correct fluid balance in our blood.

Some minerals are needed in relatively large amounts, others in minuscule quantities.

- Calcium, magnesium, phosphorus, and potassium are needed in 100s-of-milligram quantities
- Iron and zinc are needed in milligram quantities
- Iodine and selenium are needed in fractions-of-milligram quantities

But they're all essential for good health.

Iron:

- Needed for production of healthy red blood cells and carrying oxygen around the body
- A deficiency in iron can lead to anaemia
- Good animal sources – liver (the best source), kidney, red meat, chicken, eggs
- Good non-animal sources – pulses (beans and lentils), green vegetables, dried fruit (especially apricots), fortified flour

Calcium:

- Vital for building and maintaining healthy bones and teeth
- Also needed in order for nerves and muscles to function properly
- Good animal sources – dairy products, tinned fish where the bones are eaten (e.g. sardines and salmon)
- Good non-animal sources – tofu, sesame seeds, almonds, figs, kale and other green leafy vegetables, fortified flour

Phosphorus:

- Working along with calcium, and a vital part of our skeleton and teeth, phosphorus is abundant in most foods, so a deficiency is very rare
- Good animal sources – meat, fish, eggs, dairy products
- Good non-animal sources – grains, seeds, pulses, fruit and vegetables

Magnesium:

- Helps the body deal with stress and for muscle function
- Also needed for healthy bones
- Good animal sources – meat, dairy products
- Good non-animal sources – green vegetables, nuts and seeds, pulses, wholegrains, dried fruits, mushrooms

Potassium:

- Needed for the regulation of body fluid levels and controlling blood pressure
- Good non-animal sources – nuts (especially almonds and hazelnuts), sesame seeds, bananas, lentils, green leafy vegetables

Zinc:

- Vital for a healthy immune system and preventing infection
- Also needed for healthy growth and development, and sperm formation in men
- Good animal sources – oysters, meat, fish, shellfish, chicken, eggs, dairy products
- Good non-animal sources – seeds (especially pumpkin seeds), nuts, wholegrains, green leafy vegetables, beans and lentils

Selenium:

- Needed to support the immune system
- Also thought to offer protection against diseases including heart disease and cancer

- Good animal sources – meat, offal, fish, seafood, eggs
- Good non-animal sources – Brazil nuts, sesame seeds

Phytochemicals

'Phyto' is Greek for 'plant', so phytochemical literally means 'plant chemical'. These compounds are causing much excitement in the world of nutrition, thanks to their wide-ranging health benefits. Many vitamins (the ones that come from plants) are phytochemicals, but there are plenty of other examples, including:

- Allicin: an antioxidant compound found in onions, which helps protect the body's cells against harmful molecules called free radicals, thereby supporting the immune system and reducing the risk of chronic diseases such as clogged arteries, heart disease and cancer
- Isothiocyanates: found in cabbage and broccoli, these help reduce the risk of cancer
- Lycopene: another anti-cancer nutrient, found mainly in tomatoes, but also in other red fruits such as pink grapefruit and watermelon
- Betacarotene: this powerful antioxidant is what makes carrots orange – it's also found in other orange fruit and vegetables such as sweet potatoes, apricots and cantaloupe melons
- Anthocyanins: these antioxidant compounds are found in purple, blue and black fruits, such as beetroot and blueberries

Star nutrients for children's brains

Many micronutrient deficiencies (such as those in vitamins B2, B12 and C) are likely to produce brain-related symptoms, such as irritability or depression, before other, more 'visible', symptoms. So a child who eats a poor diet, high in processed foods, low in wholefoods, and low in nutrients, is likely to feel low or grumpy.

However, some vitamins and minerals are particularly important for children's brains.

B-vitamins

B-vitamins are vital in releasing energy from food, but they also seem to be important in regulating our moods. Studies have found a deficiency in B-vitamins to be associated with low mood and depression in adults, so it stands to reason that making sure children get enough of these important nutrients could help them to stay happy and contented.

Studies have shown that people who are low in vitamin B1 show symptoms of irritability, tiredness and low mood, which improves when their deficiency is addressed.

Symptoms of vitamin B3 deficiency include hyperactivity and mood swings. It's possible some children could be diagnosed with behavioural and learning problems when in fact vitamin deficiency is at least partially to blame. Vitamin B3 is also needed to make serotonin – a 'feel-good' neurotransmitter found in the brain – and melatonin, a hormone that helps us to sleep.

Like vitamin B3, Vitamin B6 is needed to make serotonin, and low serotonin levels are associated with poor mood and depression.

The B-vitamins work together, so it's not a good idea to take single B-vitamin supplements (such as vitamin B1, B6 or B12) in isolation. In fact, if your child eats a good, home-made diet, with plenty of wholegrains, lean meat, fish, eggs, dairy products and nuts and seeds, they should be getting all the B-vitamins they need.

Zinc

Along with magnesium, zinc is the most common mineral deficiency seen in children with ADHD, and numerous studies have shown that children with Developmental Delay Syndromes such as ADHD tend to have low zinc levels. One study found that one-third of the children with ADHD studied had a marked zinc deficiency that could not be accounted for solely by the amount of zinc in their diets. This suggests there could be a defect in the way these children's bodies absorb or utilise the mineral.

Some research, and practical experience at the Tinsley House Clinic, suggests that supplementation with zinc, to redress this deficiency, can help with ADHD symptoms. For more information see Chapter 13.

Zinc is also important in the senses of smell and taste, and a deficiency can dull these senses. This could be a reason why children who are low in zinc crave strong-tasting foods – like highly flavoured crisps, sweets and fizzy drinks – the very foods that will worsen their symptoms. You need to sort out the mineral deficiency, and train your child's taste buds to prefer naturally tasty foods such as fruit.

Magnesium

Low magnesium levels are associated with psychological symptoms, such as 'nerviness' and agitation, in adults as well as children. It also tends to be deficient in children (and adults) with ADHD, Tourette's syndrome and autism.

A Polish study of children with ADHD found that almost all of them (95 per cent) were deficient in magnesium, and the greater the deficiency, the more severe their symptoms. When some of the children were given magnesium supplements to restore the deficiency their symptoms improved, while those in the trial who did not receive the magnesium supplementation deteriorated.

Adequate levels of magnesium are also needed for restful sleep.

Unfortunately, today's children are unlikely to be getting enough magnesium. National dietary surveys show that the average child of six years or over fails to reach the recommended nutrient intake for the mineral. It's found in meat, dairy products, green vegetables, nuts and seeds, pulses, wholegrains, dried fruits and mushrooms.

Iron

As with magnesium, iron levels significantly lower than normal have been found in ADHD sufferers. Iron-deficiency anaemia can also contribute to problems with learning, because it causes severe fatigue, which interferes with a child's ability to work hard at their lessons (see also Chapter 10).

Vegetarian parents – Ben, aged 14 years

*Ben was born by a **forceps-assisted** delivery, leaving him somewhat battered and bruised. Ignoring this poor start, he attained all his developmental milestones on time or in advance. In fact, everything was perfect except for an ever-increasing level of **activity**. Literally from the time he could walk he was into everything and was on the go from the moment he awoke – often at the crack of dawn – until he at last succumbed to sleep late of an evening.*

At school things weren't any better, with his boisterous behaviour constantly getting him into trouble and his inability to know when to stop causing complaints from other parents whose children had felt the force of his exuberance. It was not long before Ben was being taken off to see various professionals and the suggestion was made that he should be put on Ritalin. Meanwhile, at school, his behaviour and inability to focus was impacting upon his learning and he was falling behind in his reading, spelling and maths. During the six months prior to the consultation, Ben had also developed a **facial tic**.

When I questioned Ben's mother regarding his diet, a very interesting picture unfolded. Both Ben's mother and father were vegetarians and Ben was put on a vegetarian diet from the time he was weaned. After two years on this diet Ben became increasingly fussy about what he would eat and over the years his diet basically fell apart. By now he might eat cereals for breakfast, but often he skipped breakfast and between then and his evening meal he would only eat crisps, sweets or chocolate bars. His evening meal was limited to plain pasta or cheese sandwiches.

I suggested an eating plan to firstly establish a pattern of eating and secondly to introduce the right balance of foods. I also suggested putting him on a daily dose of omegas 3 and 6, together with multivitamins and minerals, and provided some simple physical exercises to be completed at home on a daily basis. I must say I was not in the least bit confident of any measure of success; in fact, I doubted ever seeing Ben again.

One month later Ben turned up for his appointment with his mother. The omegas and vitamins were in place, as were the meal routines and the exercises. However, in terms of what was being consumed, very little had been achieved. Ben was now having cereal for breakfast most days, a cheese sandwich at lunchtime and pasta each evening. The bulk of that visit was taken up with a mini lecture on why we need a balanced diet and finally a handshake sealing an agreement that he would at least try to put in place some of the suggestions I felt were essential. Again, I cannot say I felt at all confident that I was getting through to Ben. All I could do was to give him the logic behind the dietary changes and hope he would see the need for change.

As it happened I need not have worried. When I saw Ben again some five weeks later he had more or less embraced the idea of a cooked or continental breakfast and had decided to include both eggs and fish in his diet. It was to be three months before anything like a good *diet was in place and six months before his more worrying symptoms abated, but from the time Ben decided to make the changes he was noticeably calmer, more focused and, I must say, a pleasure to be with.*

Anxious – Maggie, aged 12 years

*Maggie came into the world at 41 weeks following a long drawn-out labour due to her not engaging as she should, and then when she finally did suffering **foetal distress** as the cord was around her neck. Her first APGAR was 7 and she was whisked away for a little while before being returned to her mother having attained a respectable 9. From that point on she cried a lot and was only content if she had constant physical contact.*

*All the **developmental milestones were delayed** with the exception of bladder control. For example, sitting: 7 months, didn't crawl, walking: 14 months, single words: 16 months, two words together: 2½ years, mini sentences: 4 years. As a toddler she was a **nervous** child and was particularly frightened of strange men.*

*Once at school she struggled to learn to **read** and the build-up to **spelling** tests were a nightmare. However, her handwriting was described as neat and she was good with numbers. She was described as being **clumsy**, with **poor spatial awareness**, and a **messy eater**. She had passed through a phase of being **hyperactive** and was now calm and had a good attention span but had an appalling **short-term memory**. No OCD traits or tics were reported.*

*Maggie had previously been assessed by an educational psychologist, who thought she was mildly **dyslexic**. Her medical history included **recurrent ear infections, eczema, asthma, allergies** and **numerous accidents**.*

*On examination, all tests for cerebellar functioning indicated that the left hemisphere was under-functioning, and a computer-generated test for eye movements demonstrated **convergence failure**. Her left eye was slow to move in towards her nose for close work and failed to hold the new position. Therefore, reading would be far harder than it should be. The hearing tests performed fell in line with the history and indicated continuing middle-ear problems on the left.*

Treating Maggie proved to be far easier than I could have imagined. Her mother had already put her on a daily dose of omega-3 and

-6 since reading Is That My Child? *some two months previously, and therefore it was only a matter of tweaking the diet and providing the stair-walking and tooth-brushing exercises (see Chapter 4). When Maggie was seen again some six weeks later and retested, the results showed a great improvement and she told me she felt different in that she was not so anxious and felt happier. As the computer-generated test for convergence, although improved, was still indicating real problems, I decided to put Maggie on a computer-generated treatment programme to be completed at home on a daily basis.*

Five weeks later, when retested, there was a dramatic improvement in convergence/divergence as measured by the computer test, but more importantly her mother asked Maggie to tell me what she had told her on the way over. Maggie smiled and said, 'It feels like the path has been cleared.'

It is important to remember that, apart from generating symptoms of developmental delay, the right side of the brain, when under-functioning, can also make a child anxious, nervous or apprehensive, and this must be taken into account when assessing a child, in order to get an idea of how they are feeling and coping.

8

DUMPING THE JUNK

There are very few foods that are 'totally bad'. However, many are unhealthy if children (or any of us) eat them in anything but small quantities, and any more frequently than only very occasionally.

Unfortunately, these foods – the foods we often call 'junk foods' – often feature highly in children's diets. And many processed foods that we probably wouldn't think of as 'junk' are too high in saturated fat, sugar, salt and additives to form a *regular* part of any child's diet.

WHAT REALLY GOES INTO PROCESSED FOOD?

Sadly, profit is the priority for many food companies. And if the public buys fizzy drinks, microwave meals packed with unhealthy fats, and sugary snacks, that's what the manufacturers will make more of.

Fortunately, many food companies are smartening up their acts. And a lot of this change is due to public pressure to cut the fat, sugar, salt and additives in their ingredient lists. However, having read this book, watch the many television adverts for food products and then ask yourself, 'Are they really telling me the truth, the whole truth and nothing but the truth?'

Some 'supermarket foods' make life more convenient, without compromising good nutrition. Examples of these are tinned tomatoes, frozen fruit and vegetables, good quality low-fat salad cream and mayonnaise, fruit spreads (rather than jam), and reduced-sugar reduced-salt peanut butter (though check it doesn't contain artificial sweeteners, which should be avoided).

And unless you've got plenty of time on your hands, you won't want to make your own pasta from scratch, or boil dried beans. Provided you don't serve huge mounds of white pasta, then dried pasta and tinned beans (in water, not brine) are great time-savers, and a healthy addition to any child's diet.

When you're shopping, before you put anything in your basket or trolley, check its saturated fat, sugar, salt and additive content. Also see whether the ingredient list contains anything you wouldn't expect to see, such as a high water content in sliced meat. (You'll find more information on how to read food labels in Chapter 9.)

So what are the main nutritional 'offenders' in processed food?

Sugar

Many foods popular with children are very high in sugar, such as sweets, chocolates, fizzy drinks, biscuits, cakes, ice cream, fruit yoghurts and other desserts.

You'll also find sugar 'hidden' in many foods that don't taste sweet, such as table sauces, chutneys and pickles, non-sweetened breakfast cereals (e.g. cornflakes) and even processed meat products (where sugar can be used to 'hold' water in the meat, in order to bulk it out).

So if you're trying to cut the sugar in your child's diet, you'll need to read the labels for 'hidden' sugar, too.

Sugar traps

Obviously, foods such as sweets, chocolate, biscuits, cakes and ice cream are extremely high in sugar. But some other traditional children's favourites also deserve a dishonourable mention.

Breakfast cereals

Some breakfast cereals, including many of those marketed towards children, are alarmingly high in sugar.

For example, frosted flakes typically contain 37 per cent sugar. Another cereal promoted as healthy and wholegrain contains 21.6 per cent sugar. This means that both cereals contain over two tea-spoons of sugar per serving.

Even really healthy-sounding cereals, such as bran flakes, bran sticks and muesli, are often high in sugar – almost as high as the 'sugary' cereals. Bran flakes typically contain 22 per cent sugar, or nearly three teaspoons per serving. And children often add more sugar on top of that.

Drinks

Many fizzy drinks are horrendously high in sugar (and those that aren't generally contain artificial sweeteners, another nutritional bugbear).

A 500ml bottle of cola can contain around 55g sugar, the equiv-alent of 11 teaspoons. Even healthy-sounding fruit-juice drinks for children can be over 11 per cent sugar, which works out as nearly 5 teaspoons in one of those tiny child-sized cartons. And the sugar content of energy drinks is sky-high – where did you think the 'energy' came from? They typically contain around 18 per cent sugar, or nearly 14 teaspoons of sugar in a 380ml bottle.

A note about pure fruit juice – this is also high in sugar. Although the sugars are 'natural sugars', they still have a detrimen-tal effect on children's teeth and blood-sugar levels. This is why we recommend fruit juice is diluted half-and-half with water for children.

Yoghurts and desserts

Fruit yoghurts, and yoghurts with non-fruit flavours such as choco-late, toffee or vanilla, are generally high in sugar (or artificial sweet-eners, or both). Many manufacturers of 'children's yoghurts', alert to the fact that parents are beginning to read the food labels, are cut-ting the artificial additives from their products – but they're still high in sugar. Many children's yoghurts contain about 13 per cent sugar, which means that the Food Standards Agency classifies them as a 'high-sugar food'.

THE HEALTHIEST YOGHURT

Although low-fat, plain, natural yoghurt is the healthiest choice, some people don't like its sharp taste. If that's true for your child, you don't have to rely on bought yoghurts that may be packed full of sugar, artificial sweeteners, colourings and thickeners. You can make your own, which will be much healthier, and even more delicious!

Healthy ways to sweeten natural yoghurt:

- Add a teaspoon of runny honey
- Try a teaspoon of real maple syrup (not 'maple-flavoured' syrup)
- Add grated apple and a tablespoon of raisins
- Simmer some chopped dried fruits (apples, pears, apricots, peaches) in tea, drain and add to the yoghurt
- Add chopped or mashed bananas
- Add a handful of berry fruits (raspberries, strawberries, blackberries)
- Add a chopped kiwi fruit
- Stir in a tablespoon of chopped dried cherries and cranberries
- Stew apples with half a vanilla pod, then remove the pod when cooked and purée the apples
- Add slices of peach or pear (fresh or tinned in juice)
- Add a purée of fresh fruit (mango is delicious)

To add crunch, top the yoghurt with a tablespoon of chopped nuts, seeds, toasted coconut or oats.

Star combinations:

- Apricot and almond
- Pear and walnut
- Raspberry and coconut
- Apple and hazelnut
- Apple and cinnamon
- Maple syrup and Brazil nuts
- Honey and sunflower seeds

'Bad' fats

Many processed foods are high in the 'bad' saturated and trans (hydrogenated) fats that everyone should eat less of. Unhealthy fats not only increase children's (and adults') risk of clogged arteries and heart disease, they also crowd out the 'good fats' that are so important for health – and, importantly, for brain health. Saturated and trans fats really are the bullyboy bad fats. The good fats are crucial for children with behaviour and learning problems.

Processed meat products, ready meals, ice cream, some spreads and some desserts are generally very high in saturated and trans fats. Butter and cream, although 'natural' foods, are also very high in saturated fats.

Salt

Salt increases blood pressure, even in children. And a child whose blood pressure is rising during childhood is more likely to become an adult with dangerously high blood pressure that puts them at risk of heart disease or stroke.

You may think you don't have to worry about salt if you don't add much to your children's food, and they don't add salt at the table. But an amazing 75 per cent of the salt we eat comes from processed foods. Salt is added to foods for flavour, and as a preservative. It's also used to 'hold' water in processed meat products, to bulk them out.

You'll find salt in many non-salty, and even sweet, foods (where it is generally used as a flavour enhancer or preservative).

Some bought foods are obviously salty, such as bacon, cheese, crisps and pretzels, olives, pickles, soy sauce, stock cubes and yeast extract (e.g. Marmite and Vegemite). But you'll also find salt 'hidden' in foods such as bread, crackers, breakfast cereals, biscuits (even sweet ones), tinned spaghetti, cook-in sauces, ready-meals, baked beans, table sauces such as tomato ketchup, tinned vegetables and beans, tinned fish and soups.

How much salt do children need?

The maximum recommended salt intake for adults is 6g (equivalent to 2.4g sodium) – as children are smaller, the recommended maximum for them is lower:

- 1–3 years: maximum 2g salt a day (0.8g sodium)
- 4–6 years: maximum 3g salt a day (1.2g sodium)
- 7–10 years: maximum 5g salt a day (2g sodium)
- 11 and over: maximum 6g salt a day (2.5g sodium)

Many food labels list sodium as well as or instead of salt – this is because it's the sodium in salt that is unhealthy.

Additives

Some food additives are essential. For example, without preservatives, we'd have to change our lifestyles drastically, buying fresh food almost daily to avoid risking a nasty bout of food poisoning!

Other additives, however, are unnecessary, and are simply used to disguise food that is low quality, nutritionally poor, or both. We'll discuss additives in more detail in Chapter 12, but for now, here is an introduction to the main additive culprits.

Sweeteners

Artificial sweeteners are added to cut the calorie count of a food, but also because artificial sweeteners are a cheaper way to sweeten food than sugar.

Sweeteners such as aspartame have generated a lot of bad press regarding their safety, and although none of the scientific studies conducted to date have proven a significant health risk (by increasing cancer risk, for example), do we really want to put these chemicals into our children's bodies? Also, sweeteners do nothing to blunt a child's sweet tooth, which is what we want to achieve in the long run.

It's better to gradually wean your child off sweet tastes, choosing foods sweetened with just a little sugar, honey or fruit instead of intensely sweetened alternatives.

Colourings

Some people – especially children – are sensitive to certain artificial colourings. An ironic situation, considering that it's the foods targeted at children that are often the most luridly tinted!

These are the colourings most likely to cause problems in children: tartrazine (E102), quinoline yellow (E104), sunset yellow (E110), carmoisine (E122), ponceau 4R (E124), indigo carmine (E132) and brilliant blue (E133).

Some colourings are natural, for example E100 is a yellow colour made from turmeric. Betacarotene, the pigment that makes carrots orange, is also used to colour food.

Flavourings

Why can't food just taste like food? Flavourings are often added because not enough flavour is provided by 'real food' in the product. For example, artificial flavourings may be added to a yoghurt because there isn't much flavour due to its low fruit content.

Flavour enhancers are widely used in the food industry, mainly to bring out the flavour in a wide range of savoury and sweet foods without adding a flavour of their own. The flavour enhancer monosodium glutamate (MSG) has been found to cause symptoms including nausea, migraines, digestive problems, heart palpitations and asthma attacks in sensitive people. It can also cause headaches and numbness.

If you want to avoid artificial flavourings in your child's food, read the labels carefully.

Preservatives

Unless it is preserved, food has a very short shelf life. Sometimes it is dried, pickled, salted, frozen or canned to prevent the growth of moulds and bacteria, but most other manufactured foods will contain preservatives.

Some preservatives can cause adverse reactions in people sensitive to them. Those most likely to cause problems are:

- Sodium benzoate (E211)
- Other benzoates and parabens (E210–219)
- Sulphides (E220–228)
- Nitrates and nitrites (E249–252)

Salt and sugar are also used as preservatives.

Food additives, especially artificial colourings, have been blamed for causing behavioural problems such as ADHD. But the scientific evidence is inconclusive. Although there is a huge amount of anecdotal evidence from parents and practitioners that additive-laden junk food seems to make their children 'hyper', very few scientific studies have been carried out. The Food Standards Agency is currently conducting research into the combined effects of additives in two separate studies. One is looking at possible effects of mixtures of artificial food colourings and preservatives on the behaviour of two groups of children. The second project is investigating the effects of a group of additives thought to have common toxic effects on the liver. The results of these trials are not expected to be published until spring/autumn 2007, but in the meantime my advice is, as far as is humanly possible, eliminate as many of the 'bad' E numbers as you can. There is no doubt in my mind that the link between bad E numbers and bad brain function exists.

More research is now being carried out in this important area, but in the meantime, what can a parent do?

This much seems certain – some additives cause or exacerbate behavioural problems in some children. Until the worst offenders in terms of chemicals are identified, we have to do a bit of detective work, and figure out whether any particular foods cause problems in our own children. It's a good idea to start with those additives that seem particularly prone to causing problems – for more information, see the list above, as well as Chapter 12.

You can also minimise the artificial additives your child eats by feeding them healthy home-cooked meals, made from wholesome ingredients such as lean meat, wholegrains and pulses, and fruit and vegetables. In a recent report by the Mental Health Foundation it was stated that we each consume in the region of 4kg (8–9lb) of additives each year, and that it is not only children who are not getting enough dietary essential fatty acids. In this report it was suggested that the cocktail of additives we consume, together with insufficient intake of essential fatty acids, could be contributory factors in or the cause of ADHD, anxiety, depression, schizophrenia and Alzheimer's.

BEWARE HIDDEN ADDITIVES

Some medicines contain aspartame, as do some omega-3 preparations targeted at children.

CHEMICAL COCKTAILS

Most, if not all, of the studies conducted on additives and safety have investigated single additives in isolation. But that's not the way we eat additives – we (and our children) can consume a chemical cocktail every day, and who knows how these compounds could react together inside our bodies.

Choosing Sauces

Always read the labels before choosing sauces and dressings. Many are very high in sugar, sweeteners or 'bad' fats.

For mayonnaise and salad cream, generally speaking, the shorter the list of ingredients, the better. You should look for products without large numbers of preservatives, stabilisers, colours and E numbers. Sugar should be low on the list of ingredients, and there should be no artificial sweeteners. Any fat should be poly- or monounsaturated and the word 'hydrogenated' must not appear anywhere on the label.

For tomato ketchup, it is far better to make small quantities of fresh tomato sauce and keep them in the fridge – you'll find the recipe in this book. If you must buy tomato ketchup buy the best you can. Check the label and look for a product that is low in sugar and contains no artificial sweeteners, colours or E numbers. There should be no hydrogenated fats.

MANUFACTURERS' SNEAKY TRICKS

If you want to give your child a healthy diet, you need to be aware of the cunning ruses some food manufacturers use to part us from our money.

Incomprehensible and unhealthy ingredients lists

Avoid any food with an ingredient list that requires a degree in chemistry to understand! The most nutritious foods are those with the shortest ingredient lists, or those with no lists at all – things like fresh fruit, vegetables, fish, meat, eggs, pulses and wholegrains.

Take a look at this ingredient list, from a popular 'lunchbox' food for children. It comprises little sausages and cheese, to put into tiny buns, along with some tomato ketchup:

- Smoked sausage: pork (69%), water, pork fat, dextrose, salt, stabiliser (triphosphate, carboxy methyl cellulose, diphosphate), antioxidant (sodium ascorbate), preservative (sodium nitrite), flavouring, garlic
- Bread rolls: Wheat flour, water, dextrose, yeast, vegetable fat, emulsifiers (mono- and diglycerides of fatty acids, calcium stearoyl-2-lactylate), salt, hydrogenated vegetable fat, hydrogenated vegetable oil, vegetable oil, broad bean flour, preservatives (sorbic acid, calcium propionate), flour treatment agents (L-cysteine, ascorbic acid)
- Cheese food: Cheese (77%), concentrated whey, milk protein, emulsifying salt (sodium citrate), butter, flavouring, lactic acid, preservative (sorbic acid), anti-caking agent (soya lecithin)
- Tomato ketchup: Tomato paste (60%), spirit vinegar, glucose syrup, sugar, water, salt, modified starch, onions, spices

It doesn't look very wholesome, does it? The meat in the sausages is padded out with added water and pork fat, held in place with numerous additives.

The third ingredient in the bread rolls – dextrose – is sugar. The rolls also contain hydrogenated and partially hydrogenated vegetable oils, sources of unhealthy trans fats. As for 'cheese food' – so much of it is made from things other than cheese, they can't even *call* it cheese.

As well as all those additives, this product provides 45 per cent of a six-year-old's daily saturated-fat intake, and a shocking 60 per cent of their maximum salt intake for the day.

Certain 'functional foods'

The market for functional foods (foods with added ingredients such as omega-3 fatty acids or friendly bacteria) designed to benefit our health has been growing at an amazing pace – the market was worth around £1 billion in 2006. But do they provide enough of the added ingredient to give your child (or yourself) the health benefits you're led to expect?

For some functional foods, such as several of the cholesterol-lowering drinks containing plant sterols and stanols, the evidence is convincing at the dosages recommended. But for other products, such as several products boosted with omega-3s, or with probiotics, you'd probably need to eat an unhealthy or impractical amount in order to receive the desired benefit. For example, there is convincing evidence for the benefits of adding omega-3 essential fatty acids to children's diets. But the dosages found to provide benefits in scientific studies were much higher than the official guideline amounts for 'Joe Public'. So, in order to give your child the kind of dosages recommended by the studies (and also by this book), you'd have to feed them huge amounts of the expensive 'functional food'.

Before parting with your money, ask yourself:

- Could I achieve this health benefit with real home-made food, rather than functional food with its 'added' health benefits?
- How much of the food would my child need to eat?
- What is the science behind the claim? Did the research use higher dosages than those my child would be eating or drinking?
- Are there any unhealthy ingredients in the product, such as high levels of 'bad' fats, sugar, salt or additives?

Organic confusion

A great many people seem to be terribly confused about the word organic. It would appear that people take it to mean totally healthy and the best product to buy. Now, I have no problem with organic products other than the price we are forced to pay for them, but you should bear in mind that the organic bit only covers the period of time when the beast was on the hoof or the roots were in the ground. Once the manufacturers get hold of the beans, for example, they can add liberal amounts of sugar and salt and still quite correctly call their product organic baked beans.

The great peanut butter scandal

Peanuts are nutritious and rich in protein and fibre, and most children like peanut butter, making it a good way to get them to eat peanuts – providing they don't suffer from a nut allergy. But peanut butter is generally high in fat. Admittedly, these are 'healthy' fats, but they are still high in calories, so peanut butter packs a hefty calorific punch.

Many parents look for low-fat peanut butter, thinking it will be healthier for their children. But you need to check the label – all may not be as it seems.

When a supermarket produced a peanut butter with a dramatically lower fat content, the Food Commission decided to take a closer look. They found this wasn't peanut butter with some of the fat taken out. This was peanut butter with some of the peanut butter taken out, and a dose of glucose syrup put in its place, plus a pinch of soya protein and some maltodextrin (another sugar). This made the sugar content climb from under 4 per cent (in regular peanut butter) to over 27 per cent in this product.

The moral of the story? Check the label, to see whether you're really getting what you think you are.

Salad leaves

Have you ever wondered why, when you buy a lettuce 'loose' from the shops, it doesn't keep for long, while bagged salad leaves seem to last for ages. Until you open the bag, that is. Then the leaves go sad and limp within a day or so.

The secret is in the bag – the leaves are packaged in a special gas, which keeps them fresh.

Also, many bagged salad leaves are washed in chlorinated chemicals, and residues of these can remain on the leaves.

Re-formed meats

Avoid any meat products bearing the words 're-formed'. These are made from meat that has been finely chopped, or even 'blenderised' into 'meat sludge', and then formed into the appropriate shape. This means that poorer-quality meat or cuts you wouldn't really want to eat (and which you would otherwise spot a mile off), can be used. Some fish fingers and chicken nuggets are re-formed, as are many meat slices that are extremely similar in appearance to 'real' sliced meat. But ask yourself a simple question: have you ever seen a rectangular pig?

The 'secret' ingredients' – air and water

Many foods are actually rather low in 'food', because they're padded out with air or water. If you're a food manufacturer, ingredients don't come much cheaper than these – and who cares if the consumer isn't getting what they think they're paying for?

Low-calorie ice creams may look healthy, but how do the manufacturers cut those calories? Replacing sugar with artificial sweeteners is one way, but they can also trim the calories by incorporating more air, giving many diet ice creams an almost moussey texture that turns to nothing in your mouth. And to hold in all that air, the manufacturers have to add yet more stabilisers and other additives.

Manufacturers can also pump up the water content in meat products (including sliced meats) by adding starches, sugar and phosphates – all of these serve to hold more water in. Meat products such as sausages can be bulked out with ingredients such as rusk, vegetable oil and meat fat – all far cheaper to the manufacturer than good-quality lean meat.

Air and water aren't harmful, but they don't contribute any nutrients to your child's diet, and the additives used to hold them in place can be less than desirable.

Fruit juice drinks

Don't be misled into confusing fruit juice 'drinks' with pure juice – often the packaging is very similar. Juice drinks can be low in juice and high in sugar, sweeteners and other additives. Some of them even contain artificial flavourings. Why? Because there isn't enough real fruit juice to give them the desired taste.

Low-fat and low-sugar claims

Say you see a cereal packet proclaiming that it is '95% fat free'. Sounds impressive, doesn't it? But cereals are naturally low-fat foods – so the manufacturer isn't actually doing you any favours.

And many 'reduced-fat' foods are far from virtuous. A packet of reduced-fat crisps, for example, with a fat content of 10 per cent, isn't a low-fat food by any means. In fact, it's over three times the fat content allowed in a genuine low-fat food, as categorised by the Food Standards Agency.

Also, if you remove too much of the sugar and fat from processed foods, they tend to taste rather like cardboard. It's an undeniable fact that fat and sugar make foods taste good! So you'll find many low-fat foods are alarmingly high in sugar (or artificial sweeteners), and low-sugar foods have sky-high fat contents.

Muesli bars and 'breakfast' bars

They look healthy – after all, they contain oats, nuts, fruit and other wholesome ingredients. But don't be misled – many of these bars are as high in sugar, unhealthy fats and calories as a chocolate bar!

Hidden animal products

If you're a vegetarian, you can be caught out by animal products such as chicken or meat stock in vegetable soup and ready-meals based around vegetables, or gelatine in desserts and sweets. Check the ingredients list, and look for a 'suitable for vegetarians' flash on the product.

Flavour versus flavoured

When you buy a 'strawberry flavour jelly' you'd be forgiven for thinking strawberries were used in its manufacture. But they don't have to be. Only if the label says 'strawberry flavour*ed*' must it contain any strawberry whatsoever.

Sweeteners in savoury foods

Get used to scouring labels for artificial sweeteners, and don't forget to check savoury foods too – you'll find sweeteners in products as diverse as ketchups, pickles, instant noodles and savoury snacks.

The benefits of organic food

Try to buy organic wherever possible, to minimise the chemicals such as pesticides in your child's food. Look for the Soil Association symbol:

- Organic farmers are only allowed to use four out of the hundreds of available pesticides – and only as a last resort
- Organic regulations minimise the use of additives
- Organic foods aren't allowed to contain hydrogenated fat, the artificial sweetener aspartame or monosodium glutamate
- Organic foods aren't allowed to contain genetically modified (GM) ingredients

- Organic farmers don't use veterinary medicines on animals as a preventative measure – they only use them when animals are actually ill
- Organic chicken contains lower levels of fat than non-organic chicken
- Organic milk contains higher levels of omega-3 essential fatty acids, vitamin E and the antioxidant betacarotene

A non-organic apple can be sprayed up to 16 times with 36 different chemicals, many of which cannot be removed by washing. Government tests found pesticides in 80 per cent of non-organic apple samples.

Divorce – Simon, aged 11 years

*Simon was brought to see me by his mother, as she was very concerned about his poor school reports, the company he was keeping and his increasing level of **aggression** towards her. Before making the appointment I had asked Mrs X over the phone if she felt Simon would be **compliant**. She had said he was like Jekyll and Hyde, at one time a caring, loving child, at other times wild, angry and increasingly aggressive towards her. However, having chatted to him during one of his more amenable periods he had agreed to come and see me. Mrs X and her husband had split up three years ago and now Simon spent four days a week with her and three days with his father. She had spoken to his father about the problems she was having but had been told that Simon was fine while staying with him.*

*Once in the clinic a rather **overweight** Simon sat slumped on a stool while his mother went through his history and developmental milestones with me. Direct questions to Simon resulted in grunts initially until both his mother and I had a little go at him. Once jolted into action he proved to be a fairly articulate young man who clearly was not achieving anything like his potential. When I questioned his mother about his diet I was quite surprised to hear that in fact it was not too bad. Clearly it would require a few adjustments and the addition of some essential fatty acids, but on the whole it was not bad at all. I then asked Simon what he ate while staying with his father.*

Simon lowered his head, looked away and muttered. After the third time of asking the truth came out: burgers, chips, cola, crisps, pizza, sweets, more fizz . . .

The list came as no great surprise to me, as his weight was clearly coming from somewhere, but it clearly shocked his mother. As he was clearly a chap who enjoyed his trans fats and sugar, I asked him if he ever ate junk during the week. Again he lowered his head, looked away and fell silent. Following a verbal onslaught from his mother he confessed that he used the pocket money his father gave him to top up his diet during the week. As I could see his mother was about to blow a gasket, I intervened and suggested that it would be a good idea if Simon's father attended the next assessment, and started the examination without further delay.

Following the examination I spoke at length to Simon about the need for a healthy diet, supplements and some very simple physical exercises I wanted him to do at home on a daily basis. I again suggested to his mother before she left that having Simon's father at the next appointment would be a good thing.

Simon returned some five weeks later for his second assessment accompanied by his mother. She had spoken to his father about the diet and had got nowhere. However, Simon had taken on board the need for change and, as a first gesture of compliance, had started handing over his pocket money to his mother on returning home from his father. Now at least during the week his diet was good and the exercises had been carried out on a daily basis. In the five weeks since I had seen him last he was calmer and there had been no sign of aggression towards his mother. Having re-examined Simon I modified his exercise routine and provided him with a computer-generated programme to use at home three days a week until I saw him again in six weeks' time.

At that next visit Simon was a totally different character. He was brighter, chattier and looked a picture of health. When I commented on this a wry smile came to his face and he told me he had decided to dump the junk completely. He had apparently told his father that he was concerned about being fat and that he didn't want to eat fatty foods anymore. Amazingly, albeit after a minor outburst of anger, his father had agreed to help with the diet and when Simon next stayed with his father he was presented with home cooking straight out of Jamie Oliver's cookbook. Needless to say,

Simon never looked back: his school work steadily improved, his aggression ceased and when seen last it was in the company of his mother and father.

Being overweight can have far-reaching consequences that range from bullying, underachieving at school, behavioural problems and long-term risks of heart disease.

9

SMART SHOPPING

In order to feed your child a healthy diet, providing their body – and crucially, their brain – with all the necessary nutrients, you would ideally make virtually all of your family's food from scratch.

But this isn't possible in the real world. We lead busy lives, and often it isn't feasible to prepare a meal from basic ingredients. So, we resort to 'convenience foods'.

Convenience foods have a bad reputation – we think of junk food and fast food grabbed on the run. But food can be *convenient* and still be healthy. You can buy time-savers from the supermarket without compromising your child's diet. You just need to know what to look for, and how to read the labels.

READING THE LABELS

Traffic lights

Many companies are attempting to make labelling clearer by using a 'traffic light' system.

Traffic light labels are designed to give you an at a glance indication as to how healthy a food is. The traffic lights show you whether the food is high (red light), medium (amber light) or low (green light) in potentially harmful fat, saturated fat, salt and sugar.

For example, if you see one or more red lights on the packaging, you know that food is high in something that's not good for you.

Red = high in unhealthy substance – eat only occasionally
Amber = medium in unhealthy substance – eat some of the time
Green = low in unhealthy substance – eat most of the time

Of course, most foods will have a mixture of coloured 'lights'. A product may get a green light for fat, but an amber for sugar and a red one for salt. So you need to consider what your priorities are. If, for example, you are trying to cut all avoidable sugar from your child's diet, you'll do best to stick to foods with a green light for sugar, and avoid red and amber 'sugar lights'. It won't be such a worry for you if a food has a non-green light for fat or salt – though you should still attempt to minimise these unhealthy ingredients in your child's diet.

Traffic lights aren't perfect, but they're helpful. They give you an idea of the overall 'healthiness' of a product, depending on how many green lights it has. They can help you choose between similar products – you pick the one with the most green lights and the fewest reds. You can also see which has the 'best' colour light for sugar, fat or salt, if these are of particular concern for your child.

Ingredient lists

The ingredient list tells you what goes into a product. The ingredients are listed in order of weight, so seeing an ingredient you're trying to avoid near the front of the list should ring warning bells. This is also where you'll find out whether the food contains additives (some of which will have E numbers) and their purpose. However, where the label does not supply the additive's name as well as its E number, it can be difficult to determine what you're looking at.

Flavourings are a special case. The 4,500 or so flavourings permitted in food don't have to be listed by name – the label is simply allowed to say 'flavourings', making it impossible to know what you are really getting.

Nutritional information

Many food labels show nutritional information, which is very helpful, as it tells you how much of the important nutrients, such as fat, saturated fat, sugar or salt, is present per 100g, or per serving. Labels may also give the percentage of the GDA (Guideline Daily Amount) for various nutrients contained in a portion of that food.

The Food Standards Agency has devised some useful guidelines as to what is 'high' and 'low' in terms of the nutrients on the label. This is A LOT per 100g of food:

- 20g fat or more
- 5g saturates (saturated fat) or more
- 0.5g sodium or more
- 10g sugars or more

This is A LITTLE per 100g of food:

- 3g fat or less
- 1g saturates or less
- 0.1g sodium or less
- 2g sugars or less

Health claims

Health and nutritional claims – such as 'low in fat', 'a source of fibre' or 'promotes heart health' – can be difficult to figure out. Until recently, the law governing these claims has been very woolly, with lots of loopholes and leeway for manufacturers to interpret the guidelines in different ways. Thankfully, new European Union legislation is being introduced, to tighten up the loopholes and create consistency among products sold across the EU.

At the time of writing, manufacturers had until 2009 to phase in all of the new regulations, which include:

- Low-calorie: no more than 40kcal per 100g for foods, or 20kcal per 100ml for drinks
- Reduced-calorie: 30 per cent fewer calories than the 'standard' version
- Reduced-fat: 30 per cent less fat than the 'standard' version
- Low-fat: no more than 3g fat per 100g for solid foods, no more than 1.5g fat per 100ml for liquids (1.8g fat for semi-skimmed milk)
- Fat-free: no more than 0.5g fat per 100g or 100ml
- Reduced-sugar: 30 per cent less sugar than the 'standard' version
- Low-sugar: no more than 5g sugars per 100g for foods, no more than 2.5g sugars per 100ml for drinks
- Sugar-free: no more than 0.5g sugars per 100g or 100ml, no more than 0.4kcal per portion equivalent to 1tsp sugar, for table-top sweeteners

- No added sugars: must not contain added sugars (if sugar is naturally found in that food, the label must say 'contains naturally occurring sugars')
- Low-sodium/Low-salt: no more than 0.12g sodium per 100g or 100ml, no more than 0.3g salt per 100g or 100ml
- Very low-sodium/Very low-salt: no more than 0.04g sodium per 100g or 100ml, no more than 0.1g salt per 100g or 100ml
- Source of fibre: at least 3g fibre per 100g OR at least 1.5g fibre per 100kcal
- High-fibre: must contain at least 6g fibre per 100g OR at least 3g fibre per 100kcal
- Source of a vitamin or mineral: at least 15 per cent of the recommended daily amount of that nutrient per 100g or 100ml OR at least 15 per cent of the recommended daily amount of that nutrient per portion, if the food is a single-serve portion
- High in a vitamin or mineral: at least 30 per cent of the recommended daily amount of that nutrient per 100g or 100ml OR at least 30 per cent of the recommended daily amount of that nutrient per portion, if the food is a single-serve portion

The new rules will also mean that a food won't be able to make any actual health claims, such as 'good for your bones' or 'heart healthy' if it is unhealthily high in fat, salt or sugar. For example, a yoghurt that is high in bone-healthy calcium won't be allowed to say it's good for your bones on the label, if it is also high in unhealthy added sugars.

This is very good news – but remember that companies have until 2009 to abide by the new rules.

SALT ON THE LABEL

Chemically speaking, salt is sodium chloride, composed of an atom of sodium and an atom of chlorine for each salt molecule. It's actually the sodium in salt that's bad for you, so many food labels list sodium as well as or instead of salt – which can make things confusing.

> Here's how to figure out the salt on a label, if it isn't listed – the amount of salt is the amount of sodium x 2.5.
>
> So a packet of crisps that contains 0.8g of sodium per portion has 2g of salt per portion – which is well on the way towards the recommended maximum of 3g for a six-year-old child!

To finish off our section on labels, here are some examples of labels you *don't* want to see in your shopping trolley.

These are the ingredients in a popular cola: carbonated water, sugar, colour (caramel E150d), phosphoric acid, flavourings (including caffeine).

And this is from a diet cherry cola: carbonated water, flavourings (including caffeine), colour (caramel E150d), citric acid, sweeteners (aspartame, Acesulphame K), phosphoric acid, acidity regulator (E331), preservative (E211), tartaric acid.

As you can see, the cola is sugar-water with added acid, artificial flavourings and jitter-inducing caffeine, while the diet cola is basically water and chemicals! Both of these are very popular with children – but will almost certainly contribute to poor behaviour and concentration, and exacerbate the symptoms of Developmental Delay Syndromes.

GET YOUR CHILD INVOLVED

Shopping with kids in tow

Shopping with children may often seem like negotiating a minefield but, armed with some well-tried strategies, you can make it less stressful for you and enjoyable for them as well.

Letting children have some choice in the fruit or vegetables you buy makes them feel involved, and is a good way of encouraging them to try new fruits and vegetables.

Tips for shopping with children:

- Be enthusiastic when you spot a new fruit or vegetable you'd like them to try. If they think it is something you like eating, the chances are they won't want to miss the chance of trying it.

- Let your child help choose the vegetables for dinner or the fruit for their lunchbox.
- Teach them how to select the best and let them count out the apples or the Brussels sprouts.
- If your supermarket or deli provides 'tasters' of cheese, fruit or other healthy foods, make a point of trying what is on offer and asking them if they would like a taste. It will make them feel valued.
- Help them to become familiar with the items you buy, so you can ask them to get them from the shelves. Again, they will feel they are involved with their food.

Beating pester power:

- If you only have a little time to do the shopping, try to do it alone. Take your child when you have more time, and when the shop is less likely to be busy, so that it can become a learning experience for them.
- Consider doing your main food shop online.
- Skip the 'junk zones' filled with crisps, 'children's food', sweets and fizzy drinks.
- Don't take your child to the supermarket when they are hungry. If necessary give them a healthy snack in the car on the way, so they are less likely to pester for the first chocolate bar or packet of crisps they see.
- Make sure you have your shopping list with you. If your child asks for something that isn't on the list you can quickly say, 'It isn't on the list, so we'll think about it for another time.'
- Explain why you are buying certain foods and rejecting others. 'Because I say so' won't satisfy most children!
- If they're old enough to understand, explain to your child how marketing works. For example, pick up a mandarin yoghurt that only contains 'fruit flavouring' and no actual mandarins. Look at the label and say: 'What a swizz. Did you know they haven't put any mandarins in this? It's only orange colouring and chemical flavouring. Let's make our own with real fruit in it.'

Kids in the kitchen

A shopping trolley full of nutritious food isn't a bit of use if you can't persuade your child to eat it!

It's never too soon to start interesting your child in the food they eat. There is no need to make a big issue about it, but explain to them why particular foods are good for them, and why others should be avoided or eaten only very occasionally.

Draw an outline of the human body and draw in the brain, heart, bones, etc. Now get your child to cut out pictures of fruit, vegetables, fish, etc., and stick them around the body you have created. All you have to do now is educate your child over a period of time as to how the various foods they are eating are helping to build a healthy and happy body and mind.

Explain how things grow – it's amazing how many children, when asked 'Where do potatoes come from?' will reply, 'From the supermarket.' Let them grow a potato in a large pot or a plastic bin bag. They'll be fascinated watching it grow and hopefully will be eager to eat their own potatoes.

Be enthusiastic about new foods – let your child touch and smell new fruit and vegetables, and if they don't need cooking let them taste them raw, so your child learns not only about different tastes but also textures.

Let them help you to prepare food. They are more likely to try new foods if they have been involved. Try these ideas:

- Have a pizza-making session, or invite their friends round for a pizza-making party. Make or buy some mini pizza bases and a fresh tomato sauce and lay out a selection of healthy vegetable toppings, so they can choose their favourites to top their own pizza.
- Let them make a platter of fruit slices and a fromage frais dip or a veggie platter of crudités to dip in some healthy home-made hummus or a yoghurt and low-fat cream-cheese dip.

No bribes

Never use food as a bribe or a reward. Food should be eaten because it's yummy and good for you, not as a reward. If food becomes 'currency', it can set up all kinds of wrong attitudes in a child, making them see that particular food as much more desirable than others. If you want to reward your child, give them something totally unrelated to food, such as a trip to the cinema, or a book.

And never play one food off against another, for example by saying, 'if you eat your broccoli, you can have some chocolate'. That instantly implies that broccoli is something nasty that has to be endured in order to get a treat – chocolate.

But you need to stay strong and stay cool.

Stay strong

If your child says they're not hungry or doesn't want anything at mealtime, and you tell them 'if you don't eat anything, there's nothing until your next meal (or snack time)', don't give in and let them have a packet of crisps when they're 'starving' half an hour later. They'll know in future that your threats don't mean anything. A child won't starve just because of one missed or half-finished meal.

Stay cool

No matter how much a child tries to push all your buttons, try to stay cool. Yes, it's hard, particularly when you're tired or stressed! But if you make food into a big issue, they're more likely to use it as a way of gaining attention.

Parental Control – Alex, aged 3 years

*Alex was seen at the clinic following a desperate plea from his mother for help. Alex was **out of control** and his parents were now at their wits' end. I talked to his mother at length before seeing the young man himself, during which time I came to realise the impact his behaviour was having on his mother's health and the wedge it was driving between his parents.*

*Alex had been born at full-term following a perfect pregnancy, only to get stuck in the birth canal and require a **ventouse-assisted delivery** to pull him into the world. Not surprisingly the cone-headed new arrival was not a particularly happy chap. He was slow to latch-on, developed **colic** and had the unfortunate knack of being able to **vomit** on anyone within range. All his **developmental milestones were delayed** and after several attempts any idea of him settling into a nursery school were abandoned. At home he would only eat if fed, had to be barricaded into his bedroom at night and could only be taken out when both parents were on hand to control him.*

Clearly the examination process was going to be fun. As it turned out, once I had him fixed in my beady gaze and placed him on a stool with his knees held firmly between mine all went exceptionally well. The examination over and, to his mother's great surprise, I got a big hug and a kiss before I returned him to his father.

I then questioned his mother in a little more detail about his eating habits, his diet and exactly what they did to establish control over this very lovable rogue. It soon became clear that Alex ruled the roost, deciding what he would and wouldn't eat and throwing tantrums that would make a regimental sergeant major quake in his boots whenever anything met with his disapproval. One thing was perfectly clear – no consistent measures were in place to control this budding dictator, and the parenting styles adopted by Mum and Dad were often in conflict.

My suggested solution to the situation was to be by diet, regular family mealtimes when Alex would have to feed himself, a routine for the day's activities, a routine for bedtime and the proper use of the naughty step. As the parents and child had a lot to achieve I suggested that they – the parents – contact me by email on a weekly basis or over the phone if things were really bad. Needless to say, things did get very bad and there were several phone calls during the first two weeks of the new regime before suddenly the calls stopped. When the next weekly email arrived I breathed a sigh of relief. After two weeks of the most unbelievable behaviour, Alex had at last fallen into line and now seemed to enjoy the newfound structure in his life. It was to be another month before he finally settled down and another three months before his diet was anything like what we would hope for, but from that time on, Alex and his parents never looked back. When seen last it was apparent that before too long Alex was to have a little brother or sister, something that his parents would not have considered before.

It is very important that a child gets the same messages from both parents consistently. Never shout, and no matter how exasperated you are, never lose it in front of your child. Always make sure that when you are talking to your child you have good eye contact and that you have gone down to their level.

10

EATING FOR BALANCED BLOOD SUGAR

In order to understand which carbohydrates are best for children, and why, it's necessary to understand a little about how carbohydrates are classified.

Carbohydrates are categorised according to their structure:

- Sugars – these are subdivided into single-unit sugars (monosaccharides), and double-unit sugars (disaccharides)
- Starches – these are formed of long chains of many sugar units (polysaccharides)

Ultimately, the body's main fuel source is the single-unit sugar, glucose (indeed, it is the brain's *only* fuel source). But the body (and brain) likes its energy in a steady stream, not in fits and starts. One of the cornerstones of ensuring your child's brain functions at its full potential is maintaining stable blood sugar.

After a meal, food is digested and absorbed, and the level of glucose in the blood rises. This glucose can then be carried in the bloodstream to all the cells in the body. When the body detects that blood sugar is rising too high, it causes the pancreas to produce the hormone insulin, which squirrels glucose away in cells for use or storage, bringing the blood-sugar level back down. Unchecked, blood glucose could rise to dangerous levels, and this is what happens in untreated diabetes.

The insulin response means that blood glucose cannot rise dangerously high, but in a healthy person it still allows blood sugar to rise and fall throughout the day. However, the brain functions best when it has a steady drip-feed of glucose, not a roller coaster of highs and lows, which can lead to various nasty symptoms such as fluctuating energy levels and mood swings. It's the drip-feed effect that we're talking about when we say we want to maintain 'steady blood-sugar levels'.

When your child eats sugary foods, or highly refined starchy foods, they are quickly absorbed and result in a 'spike' in blood sugar. Your child will get a buzz of energy, and may appear 'hyper'.

But this energy buzz doesn't last. All too soon the energy will be used up, blood glucose levels will fall, and your child will start to feel hungry, tired and generally irritable. They will also probably be pleading for another sugary snack!

This boom-and-bust cycle of energy highs and lows is just what your child's brain doesn't want (though your child may disagree!). What their brain really needs is a steady supply of glucose, and this is what you get from slow-release starchy carbohydrates, such as wholemeal products (wholemeal bread, brown pasta etc.), rice (especially brown rice), and starch-rich protein foods, such as beans and lentils.

Remember:

- When your child's blood sugar rises high, they will be 'hyper'
- When it is low, they will be hungry and irritable
- When it is stable, they will be calmer

WHY IS BLOOD SUGAR SO IMPORTANT FOR THE BRAIN?

The acts of thinking, remembering and concentrating all require a lot of energy, so the brain is the most energy-hungry organ in the body. The part of the brain with the highest metabolic rate is the tiny part at the back of the brain on the inside wall that is constantly processing where you are in space. Although the brain makes up only approximately 5 per cent of a child's body weight, it uses an amazing 30 per cent of the body's 'fuel requirements' in the form of blood glucose.

> Another important thing to remember is that the brain's neurons (brain cells) can't store energy – they need a constant supply. And if a child's blood-sugar levels fall, their brain gets hungry! Although a child's body won't let the brain starve – it mobilises energy stores from elsewhere in the body – they will still experience 'hungry brain' symptoms such as feeling weak, being anxious and unable to concentrate.

Regular mealtimes

Eating regularly is important for keeping your child's blood sugar stable. Going too long without food causes a fall in blood-sugar levels, which can lead to symptoms such as tiredness, irritability and headaches.

Also, a child who is allowed to get too hungry is generally more likely to demand unhealthy sugary snacks. Regular, moderate-sized meals and healthy snacks keep children's energy levels topped up.

In terms of blood-sugar maintenance, breakfast is probably the most important meal in your child's day. When children wake up in the morning, they will have gone without food for as long as twelve hours, and their blood sugars will be at their lowest ebb. Skipping breakfast will cause blood glucose to dip even lower, leading to poor concentration, headaches, tiredness and dizziness.

To your child, mealtimes probably lack the importance they have for you. Your child probably wants to eat the minimum amount to keep you happy, enabling them to get down from the table and get on with something far more interesting – like playing, watching television or tapping away at a computer keyboard. But regular healthy pit stops are vital for every child, especially those with Developmental Delay Syndromes. That's why you'll find the eating plan in this book features three nutritious meals and two healthy snacks every day.

Unstable blood sugar and the brain

Links have been found between high sugar intake, unstable blood sugar and behavioural symptoms such as an inability to concentrate and hyperactive or even aggressive behaviour. A high-sugar diet is problematic for any child, but it is particularly disastrous for children suffering from behavioural or learning problems. This is because impaired control of blood sugar (though not as serious as that seen in diabetes) is commonly seen in children with ADHD – a study of 265 hyperactive children found that over 75 per cent of them were abnormally poor at maintaining stable blood-sugar levels.

Stimulant foods and drinks

Stimulant foods and drinks also unbalance blood sugar. The caffeine found in cola and chocolate (and also coffee and tea, though these are generally less popular with children) sets off a release of the hormone adrenaline, which kick-starts the body for action, triggering the release of more glucose into the bloodstream.

Chocolate provides a double-whammy to blood-sugar levels – not only is it high in sugar, it also contains caffeine, as well as the weaker stimulant theobromine.

You should try to cut out (or at least down) the amount of stimulants in your child's diet, especially if they suffer from symptoms of developmental delay.

Symptoms of unstable blood sugar levels include:

- Hyperactivity
- Rapidly fluctuating energy levels
- Anxiety
- Poor concentration, or a fluctuating ability to concentrate
- Mood swings
- Irritability
- Temper tantrums
- Dizziness
- Shakiness

Attacking the blood-sugar problem

Now we know the problems caused by wide and rapid fluctuations in blood-sugar levels, we can tackle them.

Here is the plan of action:

- Drastically cut the amount of refined sugar and stimulants in your child's diet

- Increase their intake of complex carbohydrates, especially wholegrains
- Feed them regular meals
- Never let them skip breakfast
- Include moderate amounts of 'good' fats in their diet (see Chapter 10)
- Increase their activity levels and exercise
- Address micronutrient deficiencies by giving them a balanced diet

---

EXERCISE AND BLOOD SUGAR

As well as keeping your child fit and helping them to maintain a healthy weight, physical activity also helps keep blood-sugar levels stable. It also stimulates the release of endorphins – 'feel-good' chemicals produced by the brain.

The problems with sugar

Children love sugar. They also eat far more of it than they should. The official guidelines are for sugar to comprise no more than 10 per cent of a child's calorie intake, but the most recent National Diet and Nutrition Survey for children found an average intake of over one-and-a-half times this.

These are the recommended daily **maximum** intakes of sugar – less is better.

Age	5–6		7–10		11–14		15–18	
	Boys	Girls	Boys	Girls	Boys	Girls	Boys	Girls
Maximum sugar	8½ tsp	7½ tsp	9½ tsp	8½ tsp	11 tsp	9 tsp	13½ tsp	10½ tsp

The amounts in the table look quite high – for example, 8½ teaspoons of sugar for a ten-year-old girl might sound a lot. But you need to remember that sugars are 'hidden' in so many foods, especially the highly refined and processed foods that feature in so many children's diets. It's not just the jam they spread on their toast and the sugar they sprinkle on their cereal.

And for what we want to achieve – trying to improve your child's behaviour, mood and learning ability – you should try to cut down the refined sugars as much as possible.

As well as playing havoc with your child's blood-sugar levels, and increasing their risk of dental decay, refined sugary foods also crowd out more nutritious foods from your child's diet. A child who is getting too high a proportion of their energy intake from sugar (as many children do) is missing out on more wholesome food, putting them at risk of deficiency in nutrients such as fibre, vitamins, minerals and, crucially, the 'healthy fats' that are so important for brain function and development.

NOT ALL SUGARS ARE 'BAD' FOR CHILDREN

Natural sugars (so-called 'intrinsic' sugars) found in fruit and the lactose (milk sugar) found in milk don't have the same harmful effects as refined sugar. In the case of fruit, for example, the fibre in the skin and flesh slows the sugar's absorption, turning it from a fast-release rocket fuel like the sugar in fizzy drinks, to a slow-release fuel of the kind the body and brain thrives on. In addition, the sugar in fruit also comes packaged with a whole host of healthy vitamins, minerals and phytochemicals. And low-fat dairy products containing lactose are also a rich source of protein and calcium.

THE BEST FRUITS FOR BLOOD-SUGAR LEVELS

Some fruits have a greater impact on blood-sugar levels than others. In general, tropical fruits (such as mangoes, bananas and pineapples) cause a more rapid increase in blood-sugar levels than fruits grown in temperate climates (such as apples and pears).

Dried fruit is high in fibre (like all fruit), but during the drying process the sugar is concentrated, so dried fruits produce a speedier rise in blood sugar than their fresh equivalents. Because of this, limit your child to small quantities of dried fruit at a time, and combine them with a little protein (such as a few nuts) to further decrease their impact on blood-sugar levels.

Sweeteners are not the answer

Although they don't have refined sugar's detrimental effect on blood-glucose levels, artificial sweeteners should not be used to replace the sweetness in your child's diet, due to their unproven safety record, and implication in behavioural and learning problems.

Also, artificial sweeteners do nothing to curb your child's sweet tooth. Children (and adults) are naturally drawn to sweetness, but it *is* possible to gradually blunt our taste for sugary foods. The more we avoid sugary foods, the easier it is to stay away from them. Artificial sweeteners just keep our hankering for extreme sweetness alive.

Cutting the sugar in your child's diet

There are plenty of simple ways to reduce the amount of sugar your child eats:

- Prepare your own food using unprocessed ingredients.
- Look for the low-sugar options if you are buying sauces, baked beans, and salad dressings (but beware artificial sweeteners in 'sugar-free' options).
- Buy tinned fruit in its own juice or apple juice rather than in syrup.
- Encourage children to drink water, milk or fresh fruit juice diluted with water instead of fizzy drinks loaded with sugar or sweeteners.

- Instead of buying cartons of ready-made desserts, mash a banana, ripe pear or some fresh berry fruits and swirl them into natural yoghurt.
- Bake your own cakes and biscuits and reduce the sugar called for in the recipe (it will not adversely affect simple recipes, particularly if they contain dried or mashed fruit).
- Mangoes, berries and other soft fresh fruit are delicious if you pop them into the blender and whiz to make a sauce. Unmould a set yoghurt onto a plate and pour over some of the sauce so that it runs down the sides.
- Keep a jar of sultanas, raisins, and chopped ready-to-eat dried fruits and a jar of nuts (almonds, Brazil nuts, hazelnuts and walnuts) handy – a tablespoon from the fruit jar and a couple of nuts from the nut jar make a good quick snack in place of sweets.
- Base desserts around fresh fruit, serving fruit after lunch and dinner and as snacks. Providing a fruit platter with different fruits cut into slices and chunks that everyone can share as a dessert at dinnertime is the perfect opportunity to introduce new fruits your child may not have encountered before. Try kiwi fruit, apricots, melon, pineapple, mango or even 'Chinese eyeballs' – lychees. Serve the platter with individual small bowls of natural yoghurt, topped with chopped nuts. Everyone can dip their fruit in their own bowl of yoghurt. You could also flavour the yoghurt with a little warmed fruit spread or stewed sweet fruit if your child finds 'plain' yoghurt too sharp.
- Use non-sugar or low-sugar toppings for crackers, rice cakes and in sandwiches – reduced-sugar peanut butter, pure-fruit spreads and reduced-sugar jam, home-made hummus, low-fat cream cheese, or a yeast extract (use sparingly, as it is high in salt). Watch out for sweeteners in peanut butter, spreads and jams.

FIND THE SUGAR

Sugar appears on labels under a number of guises. You'll notice many of them end in '-ose', and you can generally assume that any '-oses' on the label are sugars:

- Brown sugar
- Corn syrup
- High-fructose corn syrup
- Corn sweetener
- Fructose
- Maltose
- Fruit-juice concentrate
- Glucose or dextrose
- Invert sugar
- Honey
- Maltose
- Molasses
- Raw sugar
- Sucrose
- Syrup
- Malt syrup

Sugar sensitivity

Some people are believed to be 'sugar sensitive'. When these individuals consume sugary foods or highly refined carbohydrates, the food has an exaggerated impact on their blood-sugar levels.

Sugar sensitivity is as yet poorly understood, and some experts don't believe in it, but there is plenty of anecdotal evidence for its existence and the misery it can cause, as well as several high-quality scientific studies suggesting that sugar sensitivity could be behind a lot of children's heightened responses to sugar. Could your child be one of these sensitive individuals?

When a sugar-sensitive person eats sugar, not only do their blood-sugar levels rise abnormally fast, their insulin response is also excessive, so they then suffer a rapid plunge in blood sugar. This exacerbates the roller coaster of blood-sugar levels seen in *any* child after eating sugary foods.

It's thought that sugar sensitivity could have a genetic component, so if you have a very sweet tooth, and notice that sugary 'treats' give you an initial buzz that doesn't last, look out for the same in your child.

Sugar addiction

It is clearly possible to be *psychologically* 'addicted' to sugary foods – eating foods we enjoy so much (or doing any activity we really enjoy) causes the 'pleasure centre' of the brain to light up. However, some scientists believe it's possible to be *physically* 'addicted' to sugar, like a drug. Many children, especially those with Developmental Delay Syndromes, show the classic signs of addiction where sugar is concerned. They crave sugar, and become irritable and demanding when denied it.

Research on animals has shown that sugar has similar effects on the brain to opioid drugs, including heroin, by targeting the opiate receptors in the brain. Rats offered sugar-water quickly became 'addicted' to it, craving more and more of their fix, and neglecting their usual diet. When the animals were given a drug that blocked their opiate receptors (so the sugar could not bind to them and deliver its 'buzz' to the brain) they developed classic withdrawal symptoms.

Addiction and the 'child-driven diet'

Children who are fussy eaters insidiously create their own diet, often based on nothing but carbohydrates and pure sugars, the foods they enjoy. This floods the system with too much neat fuel and causes a temporary high, which the brain enjoys – this triggers a response in the brain's pleasure centre, which then craves the next high. Parents are often duped into feeding their children the foods they want and fuel the cravings by giving them crisps and high-glucose drinks. It is not unusual for children to have cereal and toast for breakfast, crisps and biscuits mid-morning, pizza and chips for lunch, more crisps, biscuits and cake mid-afternoon, and pasta for supper. All in all, a diet way too high in refined carbohydrates and sugar, paving the way to blood-sugar mayhem.

Complex carbohydrates

We now know that although the brain 'runs' on glucose, it doesn't want it in neat sugar form. So, what kind of fuel is best for the brain?

The answer is complex (starchy) carbohydrates, especially whole-grains. When it comes to providing steady, slow-release energy, the 'browner' a carbohydrate is, the better. Refining grains to make them 'white' dramatically speeds up the rate at which they hit your child's bloodstream, making them almost as detrimental to balanced blood sugar as sugar itself. Refining also strips away much of the goodness in grains, by removing much of their fibre, vitamins, minerals and protein. In many cases, refined grains are more or less pure starch.

As well as wholemeal bread, wholemeal pasta and brown rice, other good, slow-release wholegrains include millet, buckwheat and bulgur wheat. These may be unfamiliar to your child, but there's no reason why they shouldn't give them a try.

But beware. Although pasta and rice are good for you they should be provided in moderation. As the parent you should be dictating the menu for the week and this should not be unduly influenced by your children's fads and fancies. Remember, the last thing you want is for your children to insidiously cause you to provide pasta every evening.

PORRIDGE OATS

Porridge deserves a special mention as a great fuel for children. As well as providing slow-release energy to sustain your child until their next meal or snack, oats are also the grain that's highest in protein, and a great source of both sorts of fibre – heart-healthy soluble fibre, and gut-friendly insoluble fibre.

'Plain' boiled oats may not appeal to your child, but porridge can be jazzed up in many ways. Try adding:

- A sliced banana and some chopped nuts
- Some fresh or frozen blueberries – let your child mash them into the porridge to make it turn purple
- Chopped apple, for sweetness and crunch
- Stewed, puréed apple, or stewed plums, for a smoother texture
- A teaspoon of good-quality hot-chocolate powder (check the ingredients label)

- A teaspoon of honey or real maple syrup (not maple-flavoured syrup)
- A teaspoon of high-fruit jam or, preferably, pure-fruit spread

You can also make creamier tasting porridge using a mixture of milk and water. Beware some of the 'instant' oats on the market. On the plus side, many of them (especially those aimed at children) are fortified with vitamins and minerals. But because they're more 'processed' than porridge oats or rolled oats, they have a greater impact on blood-sugar levels, and some are very high in added sugar and additives such as flavourings.

Glycaemic Index and Glycaemic Load

You may well have come across the concepts of Glycaemic Index (GI) and Glycaemic Load (GL).

Glycaemic Index

In a nutshell, a food's GI is a measure of its impact on the blood-sugar level. High GI foods cause a rapid rise in blood glucose, while low GI foods cause a much slower, more sustained, increase in blood-sugar levels.

So, what your child needs for sustained energy is slow-release, low-GI foods. If they *must* eat a high-GI food, it should be eaten in combination with a low-GI food. It's the average GI of a meal that matters, so a high-GI food eaten with a low-GI food will produce a medium-GI meal (depending on the proportion of the foods eaten).

You can buy books and tables of GI and GL values, but you really don't need to bother with these if you understand the basics – it's then easy to work out for yourself whether a food has a good (low) or bad (high) Glycaemic Index.

Meat, fish, eggs, dairy foods, beans, lentils, nuts and seeds have low GI values, as do wholemeal and high-fibre foods. Most vegetables have a low GI, as do most 'temperate' fruits such as apples and pears (tropical fruits have higher GI values). Processed white foods (such as white bread, pasta, etc.) have higher GI values, and sugary foods have the highest of all, particularly those that are almost 'neat' sugar, such as sweets.

Other factors, besides its 'natural GI', also influence a food's Glycaemic Index. Basically, anything that makes a food easier for the body to digest and absorb raises its GI, so you need to concentrate on foods that the body needs time to absorb.

All of these will lower a food's Glycaemic Index (changing it for the better):

- A high fibre content – for example, much of the fibre in fruit is found in the skin, so apples eaten unpeeled have a lower Glycaemic Index than peeled apples.
- Eating fruit as fruit, rather than juice – when your child drinks juice, they're getting all the fruit sugars, without the fibre.
- 'Brown' foods, rather than 'white' – processing raises the GI by removing the fibre.
- Cooking certain foods lightly, or eating them raw (if appropriate) – for example, rice cooked so that it has a bit of 'bite' to it has a lower GI than rice cooked until it's soggy, and the same is true for vegetables (as an aside, jacket potatoes have a *higher* GI than plain boiled potatoes).
- Combining it with foods high in protein or fat – these nutrients are harder for the body to digest, so they reduce the overall Glycaemic Index of the meal. This is no excuse to overindulge in saturated or trans fats, though. Don't use the 'fat is good for GI' argument to justify a meal of chips and ice cream!

Glycaemic Load

Glycaemic Load is a slightly more sophisticated version of the Glycaemic Index concept. One problem with GI is that it gives a (bad) high GI value to several otherwise healthy foods, discouraging people from eating them. For example, sweet-tasting vegetables, such as carrots, have a high GI, because of the natural sugars they contain, and their potential to rapidly raise blood sugar. But you wouldn't class carrots as a 'high-sugar' food – you'd have to eat a huge amount of them in order to get much sugar at all.

So the concept of Glycaemic Load was introduced to take into account the *amount* of sugars a food contains. Because carrots don't contain much sugar per carrot (because they have such a high water content), they have a low (good) GL. However, white pasta is very high in starch, which the body rapidly digests to sugar. This means that white pasta has a higher (worse) GL. Pasta, in itself, isn't an unhealthy food. But the way many children eat it can be detrimental to their behaviour and ability to concentrate, thanks to its Glycaemic Load and its impact on blood sugar. In Italy, much more emphasis is placed on healthy vegetable-based sauces, served with a moderate amount of pasta. In the UK, however, we prefer a huge mound of pasta, with just a small portion of a sauce – and this is often a fatty, meat- or cream-based sauce. Hence children at the Tinsley House Clinic are usually taken off the 'heavy-on-the-pasta' type meals, with lasagne that is 'heavy-on-the-veg' being put in their place.

Quality protein

Children need an adequate intake of quality protein:

- For growth and development
- For producing neurotransmitters – the brain's communication molecules
- To help maintain stable blood-sugar levels

Because protein is slow to digest, a meal containing protein reduces and slows the food's impact on your child's blood-sugar levels. However, you shouldn't give your child too much protein late in the evening – their body needs time to digest their evening meal before they go to sleep, when body processes such as digestion slow down.

Protein tips to smooth blood-sugar levels:

- Add a few nuts to a snack of dried fruit
- If you're serving a starchy food such as rice or pasta, add some quality protein such as lean meat, fish, or a vegetarian Bolognese topping
- Add a protein topping, such as hummus, low-fat cream cheese, or cottage cheese, to crackers or oatcakes
- Make porridge with semi-skimmed milk, and add natural yoghurt
- Use lean meat, egg, or tinned fish, with salad, to make fillings for sandwiches and wraps
- Top toast with baked beans for a nutritious breakfast

CHOOSING SAUSAGES AND BACON

Sausages

Most children love sausages, but many of the sausages available in the shops are packed with unhealthy saturated fat, and are high in salt and other potentially harmful additives.

However, as an occasional treat, there's nothing wrong with giving your child good-quality sausages. You just need to know what to look for. Sausages should contain meat that is as lean as possible. As a rule, the higher the percentage of meat, the better the sausage, so look for 70 per cent or more. They will generally also contain 'rusk'. Good-quality sausages usually contain less – look for 10 per cent rusk or less. Also check the fat content – it is possible to buy sausages that are as low as 5 per cent fat.

Water forms a high proportion of low-grade sausages, and it is generally held in the sausages by chemicals called polyphosphates (described as E452 on the label). Why should you pay for water, not to mention the chemicals to keep it in?

Most sausages also contain preservatives. This is largely unavoidable – the kinds of food poisoning that can be caused by sausages that go 'off' can be very serious indeed.

Supermarket or butcher? If you have a local butcher who makes their own sausages, you can quiz them on the ingredients. Generally butchers' sausages will be high in meat, but you still need to check. In the supermarket, 'premium' sausages will have higher meat contents, and will generally use leaner (more expensive) meat, but you should nevertheless check the label for the proportions of ingredients, as well as the fat (especially saturated fat) content, and salt.

Bacon

Bacon is a high-salt food, so your child shouldn't have too much, or too often. But most children like bacon, and there's no reason why they shouldn't have it sometimes, especially if it encourages them to include some protein in their breakfast.

Quality is all-important when buying bacon. Generally, you'll do best choosing bacon from a good local butcher's, or choosing a supermarket 'premium' brand.

Unsmoked is healthier than smoked (for all foods, not just bacon). And look for 'dry-cured' rather than 'wet-cured'. Wet-cured bacon often contains a lot of added water (held in place with chemicals), which oozes out when cooked. Dry-cured bacon is generally more expensive, but you're not paying for added water – and it tastes better.

IRON DEFICIENCY AND FATIGUE

A deficiency in iron can lead to anaemia, which has symptoms of fatigue that could be mistaken for low blood sugar.

Children may develop iron deficiency if their dietary iron intake doesn't keep up with their iron needs – and growing children have high iron requirements for their size. Dietary surveys have shown that one in ten of children aged three and under, and half of teenage girls, don't eat enough iron.

If iron deficiency isn't nipped in the bud, it can progress to anaemia.

Because iron is involved in making healthy red blood cells for carrying oxygen around the body, a lack of iron can lead to a child's body being 'hungry' for oxygen. This can cause a variety of symptoms.

Iron deficient children may:

● Feel tired
● Be lethargic
● Be irritable
● Have difficulty in concentrating
● Have problems remembering things

If a child isn't getting enough iron in their diet, they may feel 'not well', but be unable to explain why, so it's important to have them checked by a doctor.

You can help prevent iron deficiency by giving your child plenty of foods high in iron (see page 81), especially if you give them foods and drinks rich in vitamin C (such as orange juice) at the same time. Vitamin C enhances the absorption of iron.

If you are giving your child a vegetarian diet, you need to be particularly careful to ensure they get enough iron, as iron from vegetarian sources is harder for the body to absorb and use than iron from animal sources.

Don't be tempted to give your child iron supplements, unless under medical supervision. Iron can build up in the body, and overdoses are dangerous and can even be fatal.

11

INCREASING THE BRAIN FATS

Fats have received a lot of bad press. Some of this is deserved. Fats are the most calorie-dense of foods. This means they can lead to children putting on weight, and obesity increases the risk of heart disease and cancer later in life.

Some fats – the saturated and trans (hydrogenated) fats – are particularly unhealthy. Both kinds increase the rate at which arteries become 'furred up', a process that can begin in childhood if an unhealthy diet is eaten. Trans fats can also hamper the proper development and function of the brain.

The table below shows the recommended maximum daily intake for total fats and saturated fats (the best recommended intake of trans fats is zero).

Age	5–6		7–10		11–14		15–18	
	Boys	Girls	Boys	Girls	Boys	Girls	Boys	Girls
Maximum total fat	66g	60g	76g	67g	85g	71g	107g	81g
Maximum saturated fat	19g	17g	21g	19g	24g	20g	30g	23g

However, the latest National Diet and Nutrition Survey of children revealed that although children's *total* fat intake doesn't exceed the recommended maximum (35 per cent of their calories) they do eat far too much saturated fat – 50 per cent more than they should.

Brain-friendly fats

However, it's wrong to be fat-phobic. We mentioned in Chapter 7 that healthy fats have a huge range of benefits, including producing energy, supplying vitamins, making hormones, protecting the body's organs, building cell membranes and keeping the skin and hair in good condition. And, of great importance since we're concerned with your child's behaviour and learning potential, healthy fats are essential for optimum brain development and function.

Excluding its water content, the brain is approximately 60 per cent fat. And – unique in the body – most of this fat is the highly unsaturated kind, notably the omega-3 and omega-6 essential fatty acids we introduced in Chapter 7.

Most of this fat is incorporated into cell membranes. Brain-cell membranes need to be flexible in order to function properly, allowing the correct substances in and out of the cell, and enabling messages to pass between cells. Flexible membranes require fluid fats in their structure, which means the polyunsaturated omega-3s and omega-6s.

Unfortunately, today's children are eating too many unhealthy saturated fats, at the expense of the healthy polyunsaturated fats the brain needs. In addition to crowding out the good fats from children's diets, bad (saturated and trans) fats also directly interfere with the brain's proper use of the good fats.

A deficiency in 'brain fats' can cause physical symptoms such as:

- Dry skin, especially if it has a rough, 'pimply' appearance
- Dry hair
- Dandruff
- Soft or brittle nails
- Itchy, dry eyes
- Raised cholesterol
- Raised blood pressure

A deficiency can also lead to 'brain-related' symptoms, including:

- Learning and behavioural difficulties
- Poor concentration
- Poor short-term memory
- Clumsiness

- Visual disturbances – 57 per cent of children attending the Tinsley House Clinic had problems bringing their eyes in towards their nose; something that is essential for close work

If your child shows any of these symptoms, they almost certainly need more omega fats in their diet.

KNOW YOUR FATS

In order to understand fats, and how different sorts are good or bad for your child's brain (and general health), it helps to understand a little about the chemical structure of the different kinds of fats.

Fats, or 'fatty acids', form long, chainlike molecules, composed of carbon atoms attached to other carbon atoms and hydrogen atoms by so-called chemical bonds. Each carbon atom has the potential to attach (bond) to four other atoms. Once it reaches this number, it is 'saturated' and cannot link up with any more atoms, and this saturation of fat molecules is responsible for the way the different kinds of fats behave, and how they are named.

The bad fats

Saturated fats

As their name suggests, these fat molecules are fully 'saturated'. Each carbon atom bonds to the maximum four other atoms in the chain. This produces straight molecules that can pack together in a close and regular formation, which is why saturated fats are generally solid at room temperature. A closely packed, more regular chemical structure is associated with solidity.

Armed with this knowledge, you can see that saturated fats are going to be the 'hard' fats like butter, lard and the fats found in meat and other products. (Most of the fat in dairy products is saturated, but takes the form of fat globules suspended in liquid.)

Trans (hydrogenated) fats

Trans fats are manufactured by the food industry. The starting point is an unsaturated fat (i.e. one where not every carbon atom has its full complement of four bonds to other molecules), which is then 'saturated', by filling up those 'gaps'. This is achieved by adding hydrogen atoms to fill the bonds – a process called hydrogenation, hence 'hydrogenated fats'.

The more an unsaturated fat is hydrogenated, the more like a saturated fat it becomes. Total hydrogenation produces a hard, waxy fat of no use to the food industry, which is why it's always 'partially hydrogenated' fats you find in foods.

Different degrees of hydrogenation are possible, producing artificial fats with different textures and properties. But they're all classed as partially hydrogenated and contain trans fats, and they're *all* harmful to your child's health.

Trans fats:

- Increase the level of the form of cholesterol (LDL) that is harmful to health
- Decrease the level of the form of cholesterol (HDL) that is beneficial to health
- Promote atherosclerosis – 'furring' of the arteries
- Increase the risk of heart disease, stroke and cancer, later in life
- **Impair brain function**

THE HOMER SIMPSON EFFECT

Being obese could contribute to cognitive decline, or 'mental slow-down'. A study gave 2,223 healthy people aged 32 to 62 four cognitive tests including word learning, then repeated the tests five years later. People of 'normal' weight (Body Mass Index 20) scored roughly the same in each test, but those who were obese (BMI 30), showed cognitive decline, faring worse in the second test. The study's authors suggest that this decline could be due to a host of factors, including atherosclerosis (the thickening and hardening of blood vessels) in the brain because of obesity, or possibly the development of insulin resistance. Consumption of saturated and trans fats is strongly linked to atherosclerosis. The 'fatness-related mental slow-down' described in the study has already been labelled the 'Homer Simpson effect' by the American media.

We have already seen above how cell membranes – especially the membranes of brain cells – contain a high proportion of unsaturated fats in their structure. These fats help give the membranes a 'semi-fluid' structure that keeps them flexible and enables the changes in shape necessary for receptors on cell membranes to receive messages from adjacent cells.

Trans fats, however, substitute themselves for the 'proper' fats in the brain's cell membranes. These more rigid fats make the membranes less flexible, hindering cell-to-cell communication in the brain.

The good fats

Monounsaturated fats

Monounsaturated fats are so named because one of the bonds in the carbon chain is a double-bond. This means that two adjacent carbon atoms use two of their four available bonds to hang on to one another, rather than just one. This double-strength bond creates a kink in the carbon chain, which means the molecules are less easy to pack together. Think of it like this: it's easier to pack straight dowelling rods in a box, than to try to fill it with knobbly, bent sticks. More gaps between the molecules means a more fluid structure – which is why monounsaturates are oils, rather than solid fats.

Monounsaturated fats include olive oil, and oils found in nuts and seeds. These are the fats with the most 'heart-healthy' reputation. They form a healthy part of your child's diet, particularly when used to replace unhealthy saturated and trans fats.

Polyunsaturated fats

While monounsaturates have just one double-bond in their structure, polyunsaturated fats have two or more.

Polyunsaturates don't have quite the same benefits for the heart and circulatory system, but they really come into their own in promoting healthy brains. The more double-bonds in a fat, the more fluid it is, and it is this fluidity found in highly unsaturated fatty acids (fats) that is so crucial in brain structure and function.

The two groups of polyunsaturates we're most interested in are the omega-3s and omega-6s (named for the position of the first double-bond in the carbon chain). A deficiency in these fats can cause physical symptoms such as dry hair and skin, and brain-related symptoms including learning and behavioural difficulties, poor concentration, poor short-term memory and clumsiness. You'll notice that these general deficiency symptoms are common in dyslexia, dyspraxia, ADD and ADHD.

Children with learning and behavioural disorders are generally found to be deficient in omega-3 and omega-6 essential fatty acids. Indeed, deficiency is common among the overall child population (and could be responsible for a lot of what is simply put down to 'naughty behaviour'), but it is particularly notable in children with Developmental Delay Syndromes. Most children could benefit from omega supplements, and these are an integral part of the Tinsley House Clinic Treatment Plan.

If your child has any of these physical or behavioural symptoms, then supplementation with omega fatty acids could improve their behaviour and learning ability, and help with any developmental delay problems.

ESSENTIAL FATTY ACIDS

If you think of the omega-3s and omega-6s as two 'families', then two particularly important EFAs called linoleic acid (LA) and alpha-linolenic acid (ALA) are found at the head of each family.

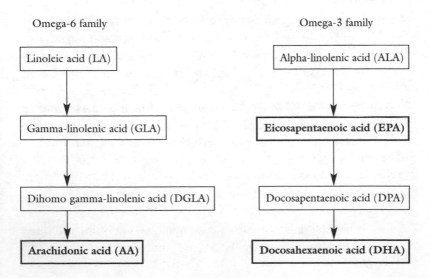

Omega-6 family

Linoleic acid (LA)

↓

Gamma-linolenic acid (GLA)

↓

Dihomo gamma-linolenic acid (DGLA)

↓

Arachidonic acid (AA)

Omega-3 family

Alpha-linolenic acid (ALA)

↓

Eicosapentaenoic acid (EPA)

↓

Docosapentaenoic acid (DPA)

↓

Docosahexaenoic acid (DHA)

The most important EFAs for your child's brain are those in bold above: AA from the omega-6 family, and EPA and DHA from the omega-3 family.

The omega-3s and omega-6s are known as 'essential fatty acids' because the body needs them to be supplied in the diet, and cannot synthesise them itself. (Strictly speaking, although ALA and LA *have* to be provided in food, the body can convert them into the other EFAs – with two provisos. Omega-3s can only make omega-3s, not omega-6s (and vice versa), and you can only move *down* the list so, for example, you cannot convert DHA into DPA.)

If your child eats enough LA and ALA then, in theory, their body can build its own supply of all other omega-3s and -6s. For example, ALA can be converted into EPA, which in turn can produce DPA, and then DHA, moving down the family.

In practice, though, it isn't that easy. In some children, the conversion from simple EFAs to the more complex ones that are critical for the brain is particularly inefficient, or they have problems incorporating the EFAs into their cell membranes. Crucially, there is a strong link between developmental delay and this inefficient conversion and incorporation. And, despite eating plenty of ALA and LA (the starting point for making all the other omegas), these children are generally still deficient in the essential brain fats.

Hindrances to efficient interconversion of EFAs:

- Poor diet, especially if deficient in vitamins B1, B3, B6, vitamin C, zinc and magnesium (zinc and magnesium deficiency is particularly common in children with developmental delay)
- An excess of saturated fats and trans (hydrogenated) fats in the diet
- Being male – boys and men are less efficient at making highly unsaturated fatty acids from ALA and LA (and Developmental Delay Syndromes are also seen more commonly in boys)
- Stress

Aids to efficient interconversion and use of EFAs:

- A healthy diet, with adequate supplies of vitamins and minerals, especially vitamins B1, B3, B6, vitamin C, zinc and magnesium

- Antioxidants – highly unsaturated fatty acids are vulnerable to oxidation (rancidity) both in foods and in the body, and antioxidants help prevent this damaging change (a particularly good antioxidant for protecting EFAs is vitamin E, so ensure your child eats vitamin E-rich foods such as nuts and seeds)

What do omega-6s do?

Omega-6 EFAs are probably best known for helping with conditions such as allergies and dry skin, but they also have an important role in the structure and function of the brain.

What do omega-3s do?

Omega-3 EFAs are important for all-round good health. They are involved in:

- Maintaining healthy levels of blood cholesterol
- Promoting a healthy heart and circulatory system
- Keeping the joints flexible
- Keeping the body's cell-to-cell communication systems working properly
- Maintaining healthy vision
- **Allowing optimal development and function of the brain and nervous system**

When it comes to brain fats, omega-3s are the real stars. These EFAs are vital for building brain cells, as well as the day-to-day functioning of the brain. Unfortunately, they are seriously lacking in many children's diets. This situation is particularly serious for the highly unsaturated fatty acids EPA and DHA. Children don't get enough in their diets (from oily fish), and generally their bodies' conversion systems aren't efficient enough to manufacture their own from the precursor, the head of the omega-3 family, alpha-linolenic acid (ALA).

> ## GETTING THE BALANCE RIGHT
>
> As well as ensuring your child has a sufficient intake of omega-3s and omega-6s, you should also try to achieve the correct balance between the two. Ideally your child should consume them in the ratio of about three omega-6 to one omega-3, but in reality the ratio consumed in this country can be as high as fifteen to one! The amount of omega-6 in the UK diet is about right – but we're sorely neglecting our omega-3 intake.

Different fats, different times, different functions

We've established that omega-3s are vital for your child's brain, but different omega-3s have more relative importance at different stages of your child's development.

Building healthy brains

Good nutrition – including sufficient EFAs – is critical before and during pregnancy, to ensure the optimal conditions and raw materials for the developing baby's brain.

The developing foetus depends totally upon its mother for nutrition. In addition, the mother's nutritional status at the time of conception also has an impact on the baby's development.

Several micronutrients are important for building healthy babies, notably:

- Folic acid
- Vitamin A (but not too much)
- Iron
- Calcium
- Zinc
- Magnesium

And, critically, an adequate intake of EFAs is also required, for the brain.

Of all of the body's organs and systems, the brain and central nervous system are perhaps the most sensitive to poor nutrition. The brain is particularly susceptible during the first few weeks after conception, when its basic structure is being formed. After this point, it is relatively well protected until approximately halfway through pregnancy, when the central nervous system (which includes the brain) undergoes another developmental spurt.

The omega-3 DHA, and the omega-6 AA, are important in the brain's structure, together making up about 20 per cent of the brain. DHA also makes up 60 per cent of the photoreceptors that pick up light in the eye and transmit messages to the brain. This means it's particularly important for expectant mothers, and women planning a baby, to get enough of these highly unsaturated fatty acids in their diet (from oily fish) or to take a supplement.

One recent study looking at expectant mothers' total intake of fish (oily fish is rich in DHA) during pregnancy found benefits from a high intake in the children's eventual language development. Another study found benefits for children's attention levels.

Pregnant women (and also children under sixteen) are advised not to eat swordfish, shark or marlin, as these large carnivorous fish can be high in pollutants such as mercury, which could harm a developing baby or child. However, expectant mums still need to ensure they get sufficient omega-3s in their diet, so they are recommended to eat up to two portions of oily fish per week, concentrating on sources that are likely to be lowest in potential contaminants, for example choosing wild or farmed salmon rather than tuna (which, of the other oily fish, is most likely to contain pollutants).

However, as far as the rest of us are concerned, we need to keep things in perspective, rather than being frightened away from oily fish by scare stories about toxins. The health benefits – for hearts and brains – far outweigh any tiny risks. And you can easily minimise your risk by avoiding shark, marlin and swordfish, not overdoing the tuna, and concentrating on the other oily fish.

Of course, supplements are another answer, and a subject we will discuss in more detail in Chapter 13. The manufacturers of good-quality omega-3 supplements ensure their fish oils come from the fish with the lowest possible levels of potentially harmful chemicals.

THE IMPACT OF ALCOHOL

Drinking more than the recommended maximum amount of alcohol during pregnancy (one or two units of alcohol a week, equivalent to one or two *small* glasses of wine) can lead to a serious condition called foetal alcohol syndrome, which can cause damage to the baby's developing nervous system, leading to mental retardation and abnormal facial features.

However, many doctors now believe that even lower alcohol intakes during pregnancy can harm the foetal nervous system, and that some children diagnosed with 'behavioural' problems are actually suffering from what is now known as Foetal Alcohol Spectrum Disorder.

The safest advice is to stop drinking alcohol once you decide to try for a baby, or as soon as you know you are pregnant.

EFAs for babies and young children

After a baby is born, the essential fatty acid called EPA becomes proportionally more significant to the child's brain than the DHA that was so important during their mother's pregnancy. Although only very small amounts of EPA are found in the brain's actual structure, it is essential for the brain's day-to-day functioning.

EPA is also used to make short-lived hormone-like chemicals called eicosanoids, which perform many functions in the brain, including releasing neurotransmitters and regulating inflammation.

GLOSSARY OF FATTY TERMS

Essential fatty acids: Omega-3s and omega-6s
Polyunsaturated fatty acids: Also known as polyunsaturates or PUFAs, this is the group of fats that includes omega-3s and omega-6s
Omega-3s: ALA, EPA and DHA are the main omega-3s
Omega-6s: LA and arachidonic acid (AA) are the main omega-6s

Alpha-linolenic acid (ALA): The simplest member of the omega-3 family, which can be used to synthesise the more complex omega-3s (albeit inefficiently)

Linoleic acid (LA): The simplest member of the omega-6 family, which can be used to synthesise the more complex omega-6s (albeit inefficiently)

Highly unsaturated fatty acids: Also known as HUFAs, these are the more complex members of the omega-3 and -6 family – in the context of this book, we're usually referring to EPA, DHA and AA when we mention HUFAs

Eicosopentanoic acid: Also known as EPA, this is the omega-3 EFA most involved in the day-to-day functioning of children's brains

Docosahexaenoic acid: Also known as DHA, this is the omega-3 EFA most involved in the building of children's brains (during their mother's pregnancy)

Essential fatty acids – the evidence

The field of research on the amazing ways in which EFAs play such an important role in children's brains and behaviour is a fascinating one, and the amount of scientific verification is accumulating all the time. Some of the trials may be biased (if there are commercial interests involved), or carried out with insufficient attention to proper scientific procedure. But, encouragingly, the evidence for the real benefits of EFAs is good.

It was the Hyperactive Children's Support Group (HACSG) who proposed the idea of a link between hyperactivity and EFAs. They noted similarities between physical symptoms seen in children suffering from hyperactivity, and the symptoms of EFA deficiency. These included abnormal thirst, eczema and asthma.

Clinical trials involving adults have shown encouraging results for EFAs used to relieve brain-related problems, including depression, and mood and sleep disturbances.

Higher levels of omega-3 EFAs have been associated with better reading and working memory in dyslexic adults. A study in the American Journal of Clinical Nutrition found a distinct link between deficiency in highly unsaturated fatty acids and ADHD. The hyper-active children suffered more from physical symptoms associated with EFA deficiency. The researchers thought ADHD might be linked to a low intake of omega-3s or an impaired ability to convert ALA into HUFAs, and concluded that omega-3 supplementation could be a useful treatment for hyperactivity.

A trial by the University of South Australia in Adelaide involved 132 children aged seven to twelve suffering from ADHD taking a supplement combining omega-3 fish oil and omega-6 evening prim-rose oil. The study found a significant reduction in ADHD symp-toms in 40 to 50 per cent of the children.

A study by Bernard Gesch and colleagues at the University of Surrey involving 231 young male offenders in a young offender insti-tution at Aylesbury found that good nutrition, particularly EFAs, can help to curb violence and antisocial behaviour. Half of the young men received pills containing vitamins, minerals and EFAs. The other half received a placebo. After nine months, the group of young men taking the supplement had committed on average 37 per cent fewer offences than those who had been receiving the placebo.

Another well-designed study supported the role of EFA defi-ciency in children with learning difficulties (mainly dyslexia and ADHD). Dr Alex Richardson and colleagues studied 41 children aged eight to twelve years, who were given either a HUFA supple-ment (containing omega-3s and omega-6s) or a placebo. After twelve weeks, the children taking the supplements had significantly fewer cognitive ('thinking') problems and saw an improvement in their ADHD symptoms.

Dr Alex Richardson's Oxford–Durham study looked at 117 chil-dren aged five to twelve suffering from dyspraxia (many of whom also showed symptoms of dyslexia and ADHD). Some of the chil-dren took a supplement containing mainly fish oils enriched with EPA, with a little GLA-rich evening primrose oil, while the rest of the children received a placebo. After three months, there was no dif-ference between the two groups for dyspraxia symptoms, but the improvements in the other DDS symptoms for the children taking the supplements were astounding. Their reading ability progressed three times faster than would be expected, and spelling progress was twice as good as expected. Their ADHD symptoms also improved greatly.

Numerous other studies have found a convincing link between lack of EFAs and DDS. Children suffering from developmental delay suffer significantly more from symptoms associated with EFA deficiency (including thirst, frequent urination, and dry hair and skin) and are also much more likely to have asthma and to have had many ear infections.

Sources of essential fatty acids

We've already mentioned that it is theoretically possible for your child's body to manufacture its own HUFAs from the simpler fatty acids alpha-linolenic acid and linoleic acid – though in practice this process is not particularly effective at the best of times, and children with developmental delay are exceptionally inefficient at these conversions.

Fortunately, conversion is not the only way for your child's brain to receive all the EFAs it needs – particularly those vital highly unsaturated fatty acids such as EPA, DHA and AA. They can all be obtained directly from food, or supplements.

Let's first look at sources, and especially food sources, of EFAs.

Omega-6s:

LA: Vegetable oils (such as corn, sunflower and safflower oil), nuts and seeds, wholegrains

GLA: Evening primrose oil, starflower or borage oil (generally only available in supplements)

AA: Meat, eggs and dairy products

Omega-3s:

ALA: Green leafy vegetables, flaxseeds, walnuts

EPA: Oily fish and other seafood

DHA: Oily fish and other seafood

(You can also buy high-omega-3 eggs, laid by chicken fed on omega-3-enriched grain)

HOW TO ENCOURAGE THE FAMILY TO EAT MORE FISH

- Always make sure you have a couple of tins of salmon, mackerel or sardines in your store cupboard so it's easily to hand when you need a quick meal.
- Get the children used to eating oily fish when they're young by including it in their favourite foods such as pizzas, jacket potatoes, and pasta dishes.
- If you can't get fresh fish, then buy frozen, but avoid fish in batter. Buy it 'nude' and make your own simple coating or topping. Everyone loves fish and chips, and if you make your own, and bake rather than fry the chips, it will be far lower in fat and just as tasty. You'll find a healthy fish-and-chips recipe later in this book.
- Try to ensure you have removed any bones in the fish before serving it to children, but also teach them to check for bones themselves (you don't need to worry about the bones in tinned fish as they are soft – and a good source of calcium).

The value of supplements

You'll notice that the HUFA we are most interested in for the purposes of improving children's behaviour and learning ability, namely EPA, is only directly available from oily fish. However, very few children eat enough oily fish, particularly not on a regular basis.

For this reason, we recommend encouraging your child to eat as much fish (especially oily fish) as you can, but to supplement their omega-3 intake with capsules or oil in liquid form. This is the only practical way for most children to consume enough of these vital fats. We'll explain more about types of supplements and dosages in Chapter 13.

12

CUTTING OUT THE NUTRITIONAL POLLUTANTS

As well as giving your child the right foods for stable blood-sugar levels and healthy amounts of 'brain fats', you also need to reduce (or cut out completely where possible) the nutritional 'pollutants' in their diets.

We briefly looked at some of these nutritional nasties in Chapter 8, but they deserve exploring in greater depth.

Additives

There are many kinds of food additives, and they are classified according to what they do. The main types are:

- Antioxidants
- Colours
- Emulsifiers, stabilisers, gelling agents and thickeners
- Flavourings and flavour enhancers
- Preservatives
- Sweeteners

What are additives for?

Additives are used for a variety of reasons:

- Improving the taste and look of food

- Keeping food safe until it is eaten
- Improving the shelf life of food
- Improving the health benefits of food (for example, by adding vitamins)
- Making food cheaper to manufacture

It's impossible to avoid additives totally. Without preservatives, for example, we would be at high risk of serious food poisoning. However, it is still possible to minimise children's consumption of additives, taking particular care to avoid the particular additives implicated in harming children's health and affecting their behaviour and learning ability.

Know your additives

Some additives are pretty innocuous.

Natural additives are substances found naturally in foods. For example, beetroot juice can be used to give a bright purple colour to foods such as sweets and desserts. Many manufacturers of foods targeted at children are waking up to the fact that parents are becoming more aware of the impact of certain additives on their children's health and behaviour, and are replacing artificial colourings with pigments such as this, that are derived from real foods.

Nature-identical additives are man-made copies of substances that occur naturally. For example, man-made vitamin C may be added to foods as an antioxidant – you'll often find it listed on the label as ascorbic acid, the chemical name for vitamin C, or E300–304. Other safe additives include E101 (vitamin B2) and E160 (carotene), used as colourings; E306–309 (tocopherols including vitamin E), another antioxidant; E440 (pectin) and E375 (niacin), both used as stabilisers; and E322 (lecithin), an emulsifier.

Artificial additives are creations of the food industry. They are not found naturally in foods, and have to be created synthetically. An example is azodicarbonamide, an additive used as a flour improver in bread.

The organic baby-food company Organix produced a list of a 'Dirty Dozen' additives that parents should avoid in their children's food.

1   Quinoline yellow (Colouring: E104)
2   Brilliant blue (Colouring: E133)
3   Sunset yellow (Colouring: E110)
4   Carmoisine (Colouring: E122)
5   Ponceau 4R (Colouring: E124)
6   Indigo carmine (Colouring: E132)
7   Artificial sweeteners
8   Monosodium glutamate (Flavour enhancer: E621)
9   Sodium benzoate (Preservative: E211)
10 Sodium dioxide (Preservative: E220)
11 High salt foods (over 0.5g sodium or 1.2g salt per 100g food)
12 Hydrogenated fat, or food containing more than 5g saturated fat per 100g

Additives and behaviour

Although sugars can be absorbed into the bloodstream within minutes, 'bad' additives can take a little longer to be absorbed, so the effects may not be so immediate. But when they do kick in, some can wreak havoc!

There's plenty of anecdotal evidence supporting the link between diet and behaviour. When children switch to healthier foods with fewer additives, there is generally a clear improvement in their behaviour. This is because certain additives are implicated in hyperactivity and a healthier diet helps the children to be more even-tempered.

The scientific evidence

For anyone in doubt as to whether additives cause hyperactivity, there is more scientific evidence from a study carried out by Professor John Warner at Southampton University.

This research studied 277 children over a period of four weeks, looking at their levels of hyperactivity. In the first week they were all given a normal diet (that is, everyday foods that may or may not contain additives). In the second week they were given an additive-free diet, in the third a diet containing colourings and preservatives, and finally a diet containing dummy (placebo) additives.

The children's parents noticed a distinct rise in levels of hyper-activity when the children were eating a diet containing additives. When the additives were withdrawn, the children's hyperactivity levels decreased.

The additives that were used in this trial were tartrazine, sunset yellow, carmoisine, ponceau 4R and sodium benzoate. What is truly amazing about this trial is that the total quantity of additives used was only 5mg per day, while it is estimated that the average child in the UK consumes in the region of 20mg a day.

Flavourings and flavour enhancers

Flavourings are often added to food that doesn't contain much of the 'real' ingredients that would give it taste. For example, a fruit juice drink that is low in real juice will need to contain artificial flavourings in order to make it taste fruity.

Over 4,500 artificial flavourings are permitted in our children's foods, but they don't have to be listed by name on the label – all you will see there is 'flavourings'.

Flavour enhancers are added to foods to make the taste they do contain seem stronger. The best-known flavour enhancer is monosodium glutamate (MSG or E621). The active ingredient in MSG is glutamic acid, or glutamate, which is naturally found in foods including Parmesan cheese, tomatoes and plums. Glutamic acid is an excitatory neurotransmitter, toxic in high doses, but it's usually consumed in sufficiently small quantities that the body can handle it. However, children who eat additive-laden diets may get too much glutamic acid (from food *plus* MSG). For most children, glutamic acid isn't a problem, but some are sensitive to it, and MSG leads to symptoms including asthma, runny nose, headaches, palpi-tations, and behavioural symptoms such as hyperactivity.

Perhaps more concerning is the fact that MSG in combination with other common additives (particularly colourings) has a 'syner-gistic' effect – the harmful impact of the additives is increased. To illustrate this, research from Dr Vyvyan Howard at Liverpool University suggests MSG *plus* the food colouring brilliant blue

(E133) had four times the inhibitory effect on the growth of immature nerve cells.

In the context of developmental delay, glutamate-containing additives have been implicated in what have been called 'glutamate storms'. That is, it would appear they trigger a cascade effect whereby excessive amounts of the excitatory neurotransmitter glutamate are liberated, resulting in hyperactive and often pointless destructive behaviour in children.

Artificial sweeteners

Artificial sweeteners are intensely sweet chemicals, with a fraction of the calories of sugar. They are commonly added to 'diet' and low-calorie foods, as well as 'diabetic' foods. Many slimmers and diabetics are misled into thinking that these fake foods are better for them, when in fact it would be far healthier for them to eat *real* food, and simply watch their sugar intake, relying on natural sugars from fruit, and only the smallest amount of refined sugar.

Artificial sweeteners are also cheaper than 'real' sugar, and for this reason they are also added to many non-diet foods, including many foods popular with children.

Their potential impact on our children's health and behaviour should not be underestimated – sweeteners have been implicated in increasing cancer risk, as well as mood swings and behavioural changes, including hyperactivity, aggression, anxiety, depression and migraine. And in addition, artificial sweeteners do nothing to dull children's taste for intensely sweet foods. To a child accustomed to fizzy drinks and sweets on demand, a crunchy apple or a juicy orange may taste 'sour'.

These are some of the artificial sweeteners commonly used in food products.

Aspartame (E951)

The most infamous of the artificial sweeteners. It has been alleged that it can cause a host of conditions including brain tumours, seizures, birth defects, multiple sclerosis and lupus. Some people report headaches and dizziness after aspartame ingestion, but the prevalence of this among the general population is unknown.

The food industry is quick to point to research that found no link between aspartame and ill health, but are you willing to risk feeding such a contentious chemical to your child? If you want to remove aspartame from your child's diet (and we recommend you try to do this, especially if they suffer from any behavioural or learning problems) you'll need to avoid labels bearing the words: aspartame, E951, Nutrasweet™, Equal™, Canderel™, Spoonful™, Benevia™, or 'contains a source of phenylalanine'.

Probably even more than MSG (another glutamate-containing additive), aspartame has been implicated in 'glutamate storms', with their resultant hyperactive behaviour.

Saccharin (E954)

Also, known as Sweet'N Low®, this is the oldest sugar substitute. It is 300 times as sweet as sugar and is a very popular tabletop sweetener. Since its discovery in 1879 it has had a chequered history, being used during both world wars, helping to compensate for sugar shortages and rationing, and in the 1970s being suspected of causing bladder cancer in laboratory animals. Depending upon which side of the fence you sit, either as manufacturer or consumer, it is either perfectly safe or can be viewed as a carcinogen.

Acesulfame K (E950)

This sweetener is often combined with other sweeteners when used as a food additive, and has been implicated with neurological symptoms such as blurred vision.

Sucralose (E955)

Also known as Splenda™, this is made from sugar in a complex multi-step process. It is 600 times as sweet as sugar, is not digested and does not raise blood-glucose levels. Based on current information, that makes it one of the best of the bunch at present.

Xylitol (E967)

This is a 'sugar-alcohol', increasingly used as a sweetener in many foods, especially sweets and chewing gum. It seems to cause fewer health problems than other artificial sweeteners, and could even help promote dental health. If you can't avoid sweeteners completely, this is probably the 'least bad' of the lot.

Colourings

Numerous high-quality scientific studies have shown improvements in children's behaviour when artificial colourings are removed from their diets. This finding appears to hold true for all children, whether or not they have been diagnosed with ADHD.

Probably the most famous research to date took as its study group a large collection of three-year-old children (only some of whom suffered from developmental delay). The researchers looked at the effects of removing five different artificial colourings from the children's diets, along with an artificial preservative. Almost as soon as the additives were removed from the children's meals and snacks, parents noticed improvements in their offspring's behaviour. But, more excitingly, when some of the children were given a glass of harmless, additive-free fruit drink every day for a week, and the rest of the group received the same drink to which the suspect chemicals had been added, the 'additive group' began to show symptoms such as poor concentration, disruptive behaviour and problems sleeping. The whole 'additives' group showed these changes in behaviour – not just those that had been diagnosed with ADHD or other related symptoms. None of the parents or children, nor the observers in the experiment, knew which drink the children were receiving, so it wasn't simply a case of the parents reporting what they expected or wanted to see. (For your interest, the colourings used in this study were tartrazine (E102), sunset yellow (E110), carmoisine (E122) and ponceau 4R (E124), and the preservative was sodium benzoate (E211).

Of all the artificial colourings, the yellow dye tartrazine (E102) is probably that most associated with behavioural problems in children. If you suspect colourings may be contributing to symptoms in your child, tartrazine is a good candidate for the top of your list of colourings to avoid.

Preservatives

Preservatives are nothing new – for thousands of years humans have added ingredients such as salt (as in salt fish and bacon) and sugar (as in jams) to food to make it last longer. Although salt and sugar are ingredients we want to decrease in children's diets, when we talk about preservatives in the context of this book, we mean the artificial chemicals added by the food industry, such as sodium benzoate, sulphur dioxide and potassium sorbate.

Sodium benzoate (E211)

Sodium benzoate is probably the most infamous of the artificial preservatives, being implicated in conditions including asthma. Also, when combined with vitamin C (also known as ascorbic acid or E300), for example in many soft drinks, it can produce benzene, which is a carcinogen (cancer-causing chemical). It is uncertain how much of a health risk benzene created in this way constitutes, but until the situation is proven either way, it seems sensible to try to remove sodium benzoate from your child's diet.

Sulphur dioxide (E220) and other sulphites

Sulphur dioxide is an extremely common preservative in food, and has been implicated in worsening asthma, and possibly cardiovascular (heart and lung) conditions. It is used in fruit salads, fruit juices, fruit-based desserts, fruit-based pie fillings, fruit spreads, soft drinks and sausage meat.

Caffeine

For some children at least, caffeine has a lot to answer for when it comes to 'behaviour issues'. Caffeine is a stimulant drug and, let's face it, this is the last thing most children need.

Some children (and adults) are particularly sensitive to caffeine, and its effects can be quite alarming. Since children are smaller than adults, the effects on them are more dramatic. If your child gets jittery or hyperactive after drinking cola, it could be a good idea to rein in their caffeine intake.

Although children are less likely to drink coffee (the most familiar source of caffeine) than adults, a can of cola can contain as much caffeine as a cup of instant coffee. Many children take in large quantities from less well-known sources, particularly cola, sports drinks and energy drinks, and chocolate.

Sources of caffeine:

- Cup of brewed coffee – 90mg caffeine
- Cup of instant coffee – 60mg caffeine
- Cup of tea – 40mg caffeine
- Can of cola – up to 70mg caffeine
- Can of energy drink – up to 70mg caffeine
- 50g chocolate bar – 10 mg caffeine
- Cup of hot chocolate – 5mg caffeine

Many painkillers and cold cures also contain caffeine, so check the label.

Advice on E numbers

The Hyperactive Children's Support Group (HACSG) UK has cited the following E numbers to which, in their opinion, children may react badly. This group of E numbers contains azo dyes and benzoate preservatives.

Their guidelines recommend that babies and young children are not given: E213–219, E310–312, E321, E421, E621–623, E627, E631 and E635.

Many children with developmental delay syndromes also suffer from eczema, asthma and recurrent infections, due to an inappropriate immune response, so it is suggested that they avoid: E102, E107, E110, E122–124, E128, E129, E151, E154, E155, E180, E211–E227, E310–E312, E321, E421, E621–623, E627, E631 and E635.

Some additives *may* be carcinogens – cancer causing – and it is suggested that the following be avoided for that reason: E110, E123, E127, E153, E249–252, E320, E321, E905, E907 and E954.

Some E numbers have been implicated in causing or aggravating problems with the kidneys and these are: E170, E252, E339–341, E385, E421, E430, E450, E452 and E541.

Finally, if you are a vegetarian you should avoid: E120, E441, E542, E910, E920, E921 and E966.

So just how do you cope with E numbers? Start off by making your own list of E numbers from those from the text and lists above and check all your food shopping. It may appear daunting but in a few weeks you will have become an expert on the foods and brands you're happy with.

Foods to look at closely for E-numbers

Biscuits, breadcrumbs, brown sauce, burgers, cakes, chicken nuggets, cola, convenience foods, crisps, cured meats, custard, desserts, fish fingers, frozen pizza, fruit products, gravy granules, hot chocolate, ice cream, instant puddings, jellies, lollies, orange squash, processed peas, Scotch eggs, soft drinks, sweets, tinned fruit, trifles, yogurts.

Top tips for avoiding additives:

- Prepare as much food as possible from fresh ingredients. In this way you can control precisely what goes into a dish – including the salt and sugar levels.
- Buy the best-quality dishes you can. For instance, choose 85 per cent meat sausages instead of 60 per cent meat sausages to minimise the amounts of fillers, binders, salt and preservatives used.
- Choose organic options certified by the Soil Association. Organic regulations are tight and minimise the use of additives.
- When you have to buy pre-prepared foods, pick those with simple ingredient lists that aren't full of chemicals.
- Take a little time to identify best options and then, in the long run, shopping becomes simpler – you know the foods you're happy to feed your child.
- Think outside the box. For example, if you want to give your child chocolate, offer them good-quality chocolate buttons (organic if possible, for the reason above) instead of coloured candy-coated buttons. Make jelly from 100 per cent fruit juice set with a gelling agent such as gelatine or vegegel, instead of using a luridly coloured packet jelly. Avoid banana 'flavoured' instant packet-mix desserts, and instead mash fresh banana with plain yoghurt.

13

ADDING THE SUPPLEMENTS

It isn't easy for a modern child's brain to get all the nutrients it needs for optimum development and function.

There is a conclusive link between deficiencies in certain nutrients and behaviour-related symptoms, such as poor concentration, hyperactivity, anxiety and fatigue. Also, children suffering from developmental delay are much more likely to suffer from nutrient deficiencies, probably due to problems with the way their bodies absorb and use these nutrients.

All children need a healthy, wholesome diet made up of 'real food' rather than sugar, salt and additive-packed processed food. However, if your child's diet has not been what it should for several years, it will take some time – several months at least – before their micronutrient reserves are topped up.

Before your child can start replenishing their micronutrient stores, they need to be eating enough of these vital compounds. Only once the body is consistently taking in all it needs for day-to-day functioning will it start to top up its reserves.

If you and your child's practitioner feel they have been eating a poor diet for some time previously, a good quality multivitamin designed for children could be a good idea as a temporary measure (say, for six months to a year). Of course, this is not intended as a substitute for a healthy diet! Also, don't be tempted to give your child supplements containing 'megadoses' of vitamins and minerals. Vitamins and minerals are good, but it's not a case of 'more is better'. Many micronutrients (notably vitamin A and iron) can build up in the body to toxic levels, particularly in children.

> When buying supplements for your child make sure they do not contain bad E numbers or artificial sweeteners.

The essential omegas

Most nutrients can be supplied in sufficient amounts by giving your child a balanced diet. However, it is virtually impossible, even with the healthiest diet, to get enough of the essential fatty acids that are so important in children's brain development and function. The only practical direct dietary sources of the highly unsaturated fatty acids EPA and DHA are oily fish, which unfortunately don't feature highly on most children's lists of favourite foods. And these healthy fats are particularly important if your child is known to have Developmental Delay Syndrome. Supporting the brain with the right nutrients will help it to develop properly, and to catch up if there has been a delay.

This is where carefully selected supplements come in.

There is now sufficient research evidence to show that a great many children would benefit from supplementing the EFAs, and further evidence would suggest that supplements may also ward off the fading memory often associated with ageing, if not Alzheimer's itself.

Children identified as having Developmental Delay Syndromes will especially benefit from having omega-3s and omega-6s added to their diet. In fact it is an absolutely essential part of the Tinsley House Clinic Treatment Plan.

Essential fatty acid dosages

The official daily recommended intake of EPA and DHA together is 300–500mg for adults. Children are smaller than adults, but they are developing rapidly, so their needs are proportionally higher. Children with developmental delay have even greater requirements.

It's probably safe to say that if your child suffers from behavioural problems of the kind we've discussed in this book – and particularly if they have been diagnosed with developmental delay –

their body stores of EFAs have been severely run down. The guideline amounts of approximately 500mg per day are only intended for 'general good health and maintenance', and at the Tinsley House Clinic we recommend a doubling of the normal dose for the first three months of supplementation, in order to build up your child's body stores of these vital fats.

Choosing a supplement:

- Make sure capsules contain enough essential fatty acids – you don't want your child to have to swallow 15 to 20 a day, which would be the case with some of the cheaper, low-dose supplements on the market.
- Check on their purity – poor-quality fish-oil supplement may be contaminated with heavy-metal pollutants such as mercury.
- Check how they are packaged. Essential fatty acids are extremely sensitive to degradation when exposed to light, so they should be packaged in dark-coloured containers.
- Heat also damages and degrades EFAs. Don't buy your supplements from a shop where they have been sitting on a shelf under the full glare of the sun (and store them in a cool place once you get them home).
- Capsules are less vulnerable to heat and light degradation than liquid oils.
- Once they 'go off', EFAs lose their health-giving properties, so throw them away if you let them go past their 'use by' date.
- Watch out for additives!

Safety note

Make sure you are buying fish oil, and not fish-*liver* oil (as in cod-liver oil). Liver, including fish liver, is extremely high in vitamin A. In order to get sufficient EPA and DHA from fish-liver oil, your child would be consuming dangerously high levels of vitamin A.

Vegetarian alternatives

Several parents have asked us if there are vegetarian alternatives to the omega fats found in fish oils. As we mentioned in Chapter 10, the brain has a particular need for the omega-3 EFAs EPA and DHA, which are only found 'ready made' in the oils in fish and seafood. However, in theory the body *can* convert alpha-linolenic acid, the 'founder member' of the omega-3 family, into the EPA and DHA so important to children's brains. Flax seeds are a rich source of alpha-linolenic acid (ALA), and if your child is a strict vegetarian, flaxseed oil (in capsule or liquid form) is the best vegetarian supplement for providing 'brain fats'.

However, the process of converting ALA to EPA and DHA is very slow and inefficient, especially in children suffering from developmental delay. If you are happy for your child to take fish-oil supplements, these are by far the best, most effective and efficient way for children to obtain enough brain-healthy essential fatty acids.

You can buy eggs and milk (and probably, soon, other products and supplements) that contain 'ready-made' EPA and DHA suitable for vegetarians, from sources such as micro-algae, but check the labelling for the actual amounts of these brain fats in each portion. In some products, your child would need to eat astronomical and impractical amounts of the food in order to receive a beneficial EFA dose.

If you do decide to go down the flaxseed oil route, you should do what you can to maximise the efficiency of the conversion from ALA to EPA and DHA, by minimising saturated and trans (hydrogenated) fats in your child's diet. You should also ensure they are not deficient in the vitamins and minerals needed for the conversion process, namely vitamins B1, B3, B6 and vitamin C, along with magnesium and zinc.

The importance of zinc

There is a marked tendency towards zinc deficiency in children diagnosed with developmental delay, especially those with ADHD symptoms. Zinc deficiency (as well as magnesium deficiency) is one of the nutrient deficiencies most commonly seen in ADHD children.

Because of this observed link between zinc deficiency and ADHD symptoms, scientists have carried out carefully monitored clinical trials to test whether zinc supplements could help ADHD children.

In a study by Akhondzadeh and colleagues in Iran, researchers looked at forty-four children aged five to eleven, divided into two groups. One group received the medication methylphenidate along with 55mg zinc sulphate (the equivalent of 15mg elemental zinc), while the other group received methylphenidate and a placebo. The children in the 'zinc group' showed a greater improvement in their symptoms than those on methylphenidate alone.

This was a randomised and double-blind study, the 'gold standard' for trials such as this. Neither the children and their parents, nor the people who distributed the 'real' zinc and the dummy supplements, knew which children were receiving the real treatment. The only people who knew were the trial organisers, and this removed the possibility of bias, by parents and children expecting to see certain results, or the people who gave them the pills unintentionally giving them hints as to whether they were getting 'real' or placebo treatment.

Another double-blind study, this time in Turkey by Bilici and colleagues, provides additional support for the role of zinc sulphate in treating children with developmental delay symptoms. This time 400 children suffering from ADHD were given either supplements containing 150mg zinc sulphate (a higher dose than in the Iranian study) or a placebo. After twelve weeks, the children receiving the zinc sulphate were less hyperactive and impulsive, and fared better in social interactions with others. This effect was particularly strong in the older (and larger) children with low levels of zinc and essential fatty acids.

Most zinc supplements available in the UK provide zinc in quantities up to 15mg. The studies utilising zinc sulphate used supplements containing up to 55mg zinc, but it is not possible to suggest dosages for individual children without knowing their nutritional status and being able to monitor their reaction to the treatment. For this reason I recommend you speak to your doctor if you feel zinc sulphate could help your child.

If your child is receiving treatment for *any* medical condition – not just developmental delay symptoms – you should speak to your doctor before starting them on any form of nutritional supplements, including those described in this book.

14

EXERCISE AND ACTIVITY

Exercise and activity are vital for *all* children. All too often today's youngsters spend their free time sitting in front of a computer screen, or listening to music, rather than running around or taking part in sporting activities.

And this kind of sedentary lifestyle is the opposite of what children need. Young bodies are built for activity, and a lack of exercise stores up health problems for the future.

Childhood is the time to form good habits – a child who enjoys being active and sporty from a young age is less likely to drop out of sports later and become a couch-potato teenager. Active children are also less likely to become overweight, and the longer a child stays overweight the more likely they are to become an overweight adult.

Health benefits of exercise for children:

- Builds strong bones, reducing the risk of osteoporosis later in life
- Builds and tones muscles (including the heart)
- Lowers cholesterol levels, reducing the risk of atherosclerosis (clogged arteries), heart disease and stroke later in life
- Lowers the risk of other chronic diseases such as cancer and type-2 diabetes later in life
- Supports the immune system – helps them stay healthy
- Helps control weight and prevent weight gain
- Helps children to sleep well

But that's not all – exercise has other, less obvious, benefits for children:

- Helps children to 'let off steam'
- Relieves stress – children get stressed too
- Improves co-ordination and flexibility
- Builds up a healthy appetite
- Gets them out in the fresh air
- Boosts self-esteem
- Teaches children the value of practice
- Team sports can teach children to work together
- Sports can help teach children to be good winners and losers

Exercise and the obesity time bomb

Many experts believe lack of exercise is a major factor behind the so-called 'obesity time bomb' among children. Approximately 23 per cent of children in the UK are overweight, and 14 per cent are obese (seriously overweight).

Why do children put on weight?

Put simply, weight gain is caused by one thing – eating more calories than you need. But nothing is ever really that simple. The amount of calories a person needs – adult or child – depends on many things, such as:

- Age
- Genes – a lot of whether you have a 'fast' or 'slow' metabolism is inherited
- Weight – big people burn more calories than small ones
- Build – muscular people burn proportionally more calories
- Activity levels – the more active you are the more calories you burn

Research studies have shown that today's children aren't eating any more than previous generations, so the fact that the number of overweight children is increasing is not a simple case of too many calories.

While their parents and grandparents listed hobbies such as football, netball, hockey and gymnastics among their pastimes, today's youngsters are far more likely to spend their spare time in front of a television or computer screen. Leisure activities have become less active, and a less active lifestyle means fewer calories are burned. If the same number of calories are going in, the result is inevitable – weight gain.

But we would never recommend putting your child on a 'slimming diet' without supervision. Here's why it would be a bad idea to cut your child's calorie intake too drastically in an attempt to lose weight quickly:

- Not enough food is eaten, so children miss out on vital nutrients, leading to deficiencies in protein (for growth and repair), vitamins and minerals
- Not enough carbohydrates are taken in to provide energy, so children feel tired and irritable
- Children will get hungry and feel deprived
- Very rapid weight loss is usually not sustainable, and is soon likely to be put back again

If a child has been eating badly and not exercising previously, simply following the exercise and diet guidelines in this book should cause the pounds to disappear. The results won't be dramatic, but they will be gradual and sustained, which is much healthier and safer.

However, if your child is overweight and still fails to lose weight despite your best efforts, you should talk to your GP, who can refer you to a dietician or registered nutritionist, to devise a healthy weight-loss plan tailored to your child's individual requirements.

How much exercise do children need?

The official recommendation is that children aged five to eighteen should take part in an hour of 'at least moderate' physical activity every day. However, approximately one-third of boys and one-third to one-half of girls do not reach this target.

The recommended hour of activity doesn't have to be all at once – you can break it into more manageable chunks, which makes it seem much less daunting.

For very young children, simply running around and playing with active toys like footballs, bicycles, hula hoops, space hoppers, Frisbees and the like are enough to give them their minimum 'hour-a-day'. Older children, however, should be encouraged to take part in some more structured exercise, as well as increasing the 'incidental' activity in their everyday lives.

To be truly fit and healthy we (children included) need a well-rounded blend of exercise. We need:

- Aerobic fitness – to build endurance and strengthen our heart and lungs
- Strength – to make exercise (and everyday activities) easier, and to increase muscle mass
- Flexibility – to improve suppleness and balance

Aerobic exercise

Aerobic exercise isn't all about leaping around in Lycra! Aerobic means 'with air', and it's also called cardiovascular exercise because, in a nutshell, it is any physical activity that exercises the heart and lungs (the cardiovascular system). In other words, it's exercise that gets the heart pumping.

For children, this could include:

- Brisk walking
- Running (athletics, or just 'running about')
- Cycling
- Swimming
- Team games, such as football, netball, rounders, cricket
- Tennis and badminton
- Ice skating and in-line skating
- Dancing

Strength exercise

Strength exercise is sometimes referred to as weight training, but it doesn't just mean lifting weights (it can include this, though weights are not generally recommended for children). Strength exercise is any activity that helps to build and strengthen the muscles that move and support the body.

For children, this could include:

- Climbing (climbing frames, hanging from monkey bars, and climbing safe trees)
- Doing handstands
- Sit-ups and press-ups (make it fun, not too serious – this isn't a grown-up's workout at the gym)
- Ballet – once your child has mastered the basics, this takes a surprising amount of strength
- Exercises using stretchy 'resistance bands' – choose bands appropriate to your child's strength

Flexibility exercise

Children are naturally bendy and stretchy, and enjoy activities that show off this ability. Most sports and active games encompass some form of flexibility exercise, as do everyday exercises like stretching up to reach a toy, or bending down to tie their shoelaces.

If your child is good at flexibility exercise, they will probably enjoy gymnastics, whether at a gymnastics club, at school gym classes or simply performing cartwheels or bending over backwards to make a 'crab' in the garden.

Building healthy muscles

All too often, as children grow they put on more fat than they should, at the expense of muscular tissue.

Children who put on fat are likely to grow fatter, because fat is 'metabolically inactive'. Basically, it just sits there. In contrast, muscle tissue is metabolically active – it has to burn calories simply to exist, and not just when the child is exercising.

Therefore, a child with a high proportion of body fat will burn fewer calories than a child who has less fat (and more muscle), even if the two children weigh exactly the same, and take just the same amount of exercise.

How do you ensure your child grows in terms of muscle, not fat? The answer is simple – a healthy diet, and plenty of physical activity.

Weight-bearing exercise

At least twice a week children should take part in activities that will help build their bones – so-called 'weight bearing exercise'. This is because the years of rapid growth during childhood and young adulthood are the best time to build bone density.

Any exercise that involves standing up and moving about counts as weight-bearing. Good examples for children include:

- Walking
- Running
- Skipping
- Tennis
- Football
- Netball
- Hockey
- Trampolining

SAFETY FIRST

Ensure your child has all the necessary clothing and safety equipment for their sport, such as trainers for running, a helmet for cycling, elbow and knee pads for skating and the proper outfit for judo.

Set a good example

Show your child you think exercise is important by being active yourself. Make fitness a family affair – every one of us needs exercise, and research has shown that parents who enjoy physical activity themselves are more likely to encourage their children to be active. Try to plan at least one family activity each week – it doesn't need to be expensive or even cost anything at all.

Try:
- A hike in the country
- A climb up a local hill
- A visit to a playground
- A visit to a stately home – explore the house and grounds
- A treasure hunt in the house or garden

- A game of cricket or football in the park
- A walk along a river or a trip to the beach (beach games in winter are great fun and the sands are less crowded)
- Making an obstacle course in the garden
- Flying a kite
- A visit to an ice rink
- A trip to the local swimming pool
- A cycle ride
- Family 'orienteering' – in other words, a walk following a map
- If it's a wet afternoon, put on some music and dance

Incorporate activity into your daily life. There are plenty of ways to boost activity levels, without it seeming like 'actual exercise'.

These are just a few suggestions, which will be appropriate for children of different ages.

- Walking to the shops if it's not too far
- Walking to school, if it's not too far
- Using the stairs rather than a lift or escalator wherever possible
- Letting them walk the dog with you if you have one
- Tidying their own room and helping around the house
- Helping in the garden, for example sweeping or gathering up leaves
- Having their own little garden plot to cultivate
- Helping to wash the car

Sports and clubs

If your child is old enough, sports clubs are a great way to enable them to exercise in a safe and supportive environment, surrounded by fellow enthusiasts, and coached by experts. If you are a member of a sports club yourself, they may offer junior membership, so you can encourage your child in your shared interest.

If your child is the competitive type, they will probably love the opportunity to compete against their peers, and rise through the ranks in 'graded' sports such as judo and karate. But don't allow anyone – yourself included – to put pressure on your child to excel.

This is particularly important for younger children, who may not be emotionally ready for the potential stress and disappointment of competition.

Unless you are confident your child can take it, be cautious of clubs who require them to pass 'tests' or take part in 'trials' before they can join. Beware if the emphasis seems to be on 'winning' and travelling around attending competitions rather than the enjoyment of participating. And if your child appears to be growing obsessive or overly driven where their chosen sport is concerned, tell their teacher or trainer about your concerns. Above all, exercise should be fun.

CHECK IT OUT

Before you enrol your child in any physical activity class or sports club you should satisfy yourself that the coaching staff or teachers are qualified to teach their age group. Go along with your child to watch a session before they join, so you can watch the trainers in action and be satisfied that they encourage and praise all of the participants – not only the most able. Children need support and encouragement as well as instruction if they are to get the maximum benefit from any activity.

You also need to be sure that all of the children are given a chance to get involved and that some don't spend most of their time sitting out on the bench – there's no fun in that. And if your child doesn't like the teacher, for whatever reason, don't try to cajole them into attending.

Don't push children into activities they don't seem ready for. Children develop at different speeds and need to be allowed to progress at their own rates. You will find their interests change as they grow older and they may want to move on to different activities and sports along the way. The most important thing is that they actually do some exercise, not what it is.

HELPFUL TIPS FOR AN ACTIVE CHILD

Start them young, with a variety of activities appropriate to their age. It's easier to maintain an active lifestyle, adapting it as your children grow older, than to spring exercise on them when they are older and unfit.

- Help your child to choose sports they enjoy. Find activities they excel in – every child can be good at something.
- Try your local library for information on local sports clubs and classes. Schools and sports centres often run a good range.
- Don't rule out more unusual sports, like martial arts, trampolining, dance or horse riding.
- Establish a regular schedule for physical activity – exercise is a healthy habit.
- Embrace a more active lifestyle yourself, so you'll be a positive role model for your child.
- For older children, why not try doing something a little scary together? It is a great way to gain respect.
- Above all, keep it fun. Then your child will keep coming back for more.

Hydration for active children

Dehydration is particularly serious for children. Because of their larger surface areas relative to their size, they lose water more rapidly. Active children need extra water, and they should be encouraged to drink water before, during (take frequent water breaks) and after exercise. You can also help prevent your child from becoming overheated (which increases the rate of fluid loss) by avoiding exercise during the hottest period of the day (between 10 a.m. and 3 p.m.), and ensuring they wear loose-fitting clothing (appropriate to the type of exercise) that can 'breathe'.

Look out for the symptoms of dehydration when your child is exercising or simply playing or running about a lot, particularly if it is a hot day, or they are in a warm building. If your child complains of a headache, feels sick, weak, dizzy, excessively tired, or they develop muscle cramps, these could be the early signs of dehydration, meaning that it's time to stop and take a drink. Encourage your child to take small sips, rather than gulping down a large amount of water quickly.

It's also important that your child knows these symptoms are signs of potential trouble, so they can tell their trainer or teacher if they occur when you are not there. Other symptoms to watch out for are pale skin and/or a rapid heartbeat.

EXERCISE FOR CHILDREN WITH DEVELOPMENTAL DELAY SYNDROMES

If your child has a DDS, particularly if they show symptoms of dyspraxia, ADD or ADHD, they may find 'formal' exercise difficult, frustrating or embarrassing. If this is the case, try the simple exercises in Chapter 4 and note any improvements that follow in terms of general co-ordination, balance and hand/eye co-ordination. You may need to seek specialist advice if you don't see any improvement over a six-week period.

Remember, you should always encourage your child to be active, whatever their abilities.

15

THE IMPORTANCE OF SLEEP

Being tired during the day puts a dampener on anyone's quality of life – and children aren't immune.

Getting sufficient sleep is vital for children as it directly impacts upon both their mental and physical development. Research also suggests that lack of sleep can disrupt the production of the 'hunger hormone' ghrelin, leading to an increased desire for food, which can contribute to obesity.

As children grow up, though, they need less sleep:

- 3–5 years old – average 11–13 hours
- 6–12 years – average 10–11 hours

However, there is great variability between the amount of sleep individual children need. Your friend's ten-year-old may manage perfectly well on seven hours' sleep, but your own child might feel horrendously sleepy unless they get eight hours.

A lack of sleep can lead to a variety of symptoms:

- Excessive problems waking up in the morning
- Tiredness during the day
- Irritability
- Problems concentrating
- A weakened immune system, leading to reduced resistance to infections

It's obvious that tiredness and lack of concentration will stop children fulfilling their potential at school, both in academic subjects and physical activity. Sleeplessness can also lead to low mood and depression – it's no fun always being tired. Aggression can be the result of frustration caused by tiredness.

Helping school-age children get enough sleep can be tricky. At this age they may be finding schoolwork and homework stressful, computers and the Internet become fascinating, and they believe fizzy caffeinated drinks are *the* thing to drink.

However, there's a lot you can do regarding your child's routine, and also their diet, to help them get the restful sleep they need.

Sleep advice for children

Stress
Stress and excitement during the evening can prevent a child from getting to sleep. Children, particularly those with developmental delay, thrive on security. What they need is a familiar and reassuring 'winding down routine'. This will vary according to the child's age, but could run like this: homework (if applicable), supper, TV, bath, pyjamas, teeth-cleaning, reading or bedtime story, followed by 'lights out'.

Televisions and computers
Try to keep computers and televisions out of your child's room, as they play havoc with the winding-down process you are trying to encourage. If this is unavoidable, they should not be switched on after supper, or after a set time for older children. Certainly don't leave your child to 'drop off' to sleep with the television on – a study of nearly 500 children in America found that television watching at bedtime was the strongest predictor of children having problems getting to sleep, and waking in the night.

Tire them out!
Plenty of activity earlier in the day, however, helps children get to sleep at night. Children who don't get enough exercise are more likely to have problems sleeping.

Caffeine

When it comes to food and drink, caffeine is the worst possible thing for your child's sleep prospects. Caffeinated drinks such as coffee and cola are things we discourage for children. Try to stop your child from drinking caffeinated drinks after lunchtime, and certainly not in the evening. Also, it takes time for the effects of caffeine to clear from your child's system. If they are consistently topping up with caffeinated drinks and chocolate through the day, they will still be 'caffeinated' at bedtime. Children's sensitivity to caffeine varies – for some children, even a small amount early in the day will keep them awake at night.

Some useful guidelines for children's maximum caffeine intakes, from Health Canada, are:

- 45mg for children aged 4–6
- 62.5mg for children aged 7–9
- 85mg for children aged 10–12

A can of cola, a cup of tea or a small (50g) bar of dark chocolate each contain approximately 50mg of caffeine. With many children in the UK consuming several times more than this, it's not difficulty to see why they have difficulty sleeping.

Late meals

Don't give your child their supper too close to bedtime. A main meal takes time to digest, and late suppers hamper both your child's digestion and ability to get to sleep.

However, a bedtime snack containing slow-release carbohydrates, such as a cup of hot milk and an oatcake or a banana, can be fitted into the bedtime routine, just before teeth-cleaning, and can help a child get to sleep.

Think about blood sugar

Chaotic blood-sugar levels can also hinder a child's ability to get to sleep, and stay asleep through the night. Sugary foods eaten in the evening can make a child 'buzzy' and unable to settle down. Conversely, being too hungry can also make it difficult to sleep, so consider giving your child a healthy bedtime snack.

Sleepy foods

Certain nutrients and foods are believed to help promote restful sleep.

A lack of **magnesium** is associated with difficulty in sleeping, and also with developmental delay symptoms. Good sources of this mineral include green leafy vegetables, beans, pulses and nuts.

The high **calcium** content of milk is thought to be one of the reasons for recommending a milky drink at bedtime. Other good sources of calcium include other low-fat dairy products, tinned sardines and salmon, and tofu.

B-vitamins help your child deal with stress and anxiety, which are often a cause of insomnia. Make sure their diet is rich in B-vitamins from healthy sources such as nuts, seeds, pulses, eggs, molasses, wholegrains and yeast extract.

SLEEPY TIPS

- Don't creep around like mice when your child has gone to bed. A little background noise will reassure them you are still there and all is well.
- Make sure your child's room is a comfortable temperature for sleep, with no draughts.
- Don't let your child drink too much fluid in the few hours before they go to bed. Having to get up during the night to visit the bathroom will disturb their sleep.

Children with a level of hyperactivity often find it difficult to wind down at the end of the day and therefore have problems getting off to sleep. Do not make the mistake of letting them stay up late, as this will only leave them tired and grumpy in the morning. It is essential that these children in particular have a set routine and a fixed bedtime.

Children with developmental delay have problems particularly in the right side of the brain. As the right side of the brain is all to do with approach/withdrawal, when it under-functions everything can seem a bit scary. Therefore, it is not unusual for children with developmental delay to wake in the night due to the noises that all houses make or the wind howling outside, and end up in bed with Mum. To help with this scenario there are specially designed BrainBalance CDs that can be played discreetly in the background. Visit www.i-waveonline.com for further information.

The holistic approach – Jordan, aged 8 years

Before attending Tinsley House Clinic Jordan had spent a year doing daily exercises to improve the functioning of his cerebellum, having been assessed at a centre specialising in the treatment of dyslexia. Initially he had shown signs of improvement in that, when assessed at the centre he was attending, his balance and eye movements (not convergence) were measurably better, but in terms of his problems at home and at school nothing had changed. In fact, at home things were getting increasingly fraught, with ever-increasing resistance to doing the daily exercise chore.

*From the case history it was apparent that Jordan was falling further and further behind at school, was increasingly struggling with his **reading**, had a very short **attention span**, a poor **short-term memory** and was a **fidget** to say the least. His **diet** was self-imposed and appalling and his mother had been advised **not** to give him any supplements. Once the examination was complete, one thing became very clear – his left eye consistently failed to converge (move in towards the nose). Accommodation/convergence failure is seen in 57 per cent of the children attending Tinsley House and is, I believe, a common cause of the misdiagnosis of dyslexia. Jordan was struggling to read due to the convergence failure and this in turn was leading to lack of attention and increasing frustration.*

I talked to Jordan about his diet and why I felt we needed to make some changes, and suggested he should take a double dose of omega-3 and -6 for three months, together with some vitamins and minerals to address any deficiency. I also provided a computer-generated programme to treat the convergence failure. As Jordan was sick to death of physical exercises I suggested to him that he should teach his family how to do a brain exercise I call 'double doodles'. From that time on, Jordan never looked back. At each visit his ability to converge his eyes was tested using a computer-generated test programme that measures convergence/divergence in diopters. His diet slowly changed and, over a period of weeks, it became very healthy. After five months of treatment his reading was age-appropriate, he could settle down and concentrate on his work without fidgeting constantly, and best of all his self-esteem was rocketing.

Exercise alone is not enough. To be successful, a holistic approach is necessary where diet, supplementation, exercise and treatments aimed at specific areas of the brain are employed. As the majority of symptoms of developmental delay originate in the right prefrontal cortex, cerebellar-based exercises alone (although a good starting point) are not the answer. Also, not testing for something as common as convergence failure is a very basic error.

16

THE SMART BRAIN DIET

The previous chapters in this book explain the nutrients children need, and the foods that are the best for supplying them. This chapter sets out a 14-day eating plan designed for *any* child, but that would be especially beneficial for children with developmental delay symptoms. It's certainly not a 'diet' in the weight-loss sense of the word. Rather, it's a healthy eating plan, paying particular attention to the nutrients needed to fulfil their learning potential, and cutting out the pollutants implicated in behavioural symptoms.

You will probably have to adjust portion sizes according to your child's age, sex and activity levels. Once you have cut the 'junk food' out of your child's diet, you'll almost certainly notice they can eat a lot more food without putting on weight. Healthy wholefoods, of the kind we recommend, are higher in nutrients and generally lower in calories and fat than unhealthy processed food.

If your child is hungry on the eating plan, or they lose weight (and don't need to), then allow them slightly larger portions of the wholegrain carbohydrates and protein. For example, give them a two-egg scrambled egg or omelette, or a slightly larger portion of chicken. Allow two slices of wholemeal toast with their baked beans. Or add an oatcake to their snack of veggie sticks and a dip. If you're uncertain, or if your child has special nutritional needs (for example, they have a food allergy, are diabetic or are vegetarian) show this book to your child's GP, practitioner or a registered nutritionist, so you can explain what you are trying to achieve, and ask them to advise you on portion sizes and adapting the plan to suit your child.

However, it is very important to stick to the plan. Deciding to let your child 'have a day off', giving in to the occasional plea for a bottle of cola, or going back to your old ways for Christmas or a holiday, will undo all your efforts. And if your child doesn't quickly notice any payback from the eating plan, they may well decide that this 'diet thing' isn't worth the bother.

But once your child begins to see the positive benefits of their new way of eating, they will hopefully become its greatest advocate.

After completing the 14-day plan, you will hopefully be seeing improvements in your child's behaviour, symptoms and general health. You can still continue to use meals and snacks from the plan after this, but we have also provided (in Chapter 19) guidelines on how to adapt the diet plan for the long term.

These are the main points behind the 14-day plan:

- Regular mealtimes
- Cut out simple sugars as far as possible
- Reduce simple carbohydrates (such as white pasta and white bread)
- The special importance of breakfast
- Healthy snacks to balance blood sugar
- Dump the junk and processed food (to reduce harmful fats and additives)
- Increase omega-3s and omega-6s (through diet and supplements)
- Possibly introduce zinc sulphate supplements
- Eat together – share the food and the company

MEALTIMES AND MEALS

It's important for your child to have regular meals and snacks, spaced throughout the day. This will help keep them sustained and contented, and their blood-sugar levels stable.

Breakfast

Although other meals may provide more of the 'brain fats' and other nutrients your child needs, in terms of its immediate impact on children's performance at school, breakfast is the *most important* meal of the day.

A good breakfast of the kind we recommend sets a child up for the day, supplying them with slow-release energy to sustain them through the morning. A 'bad' breakfast, packed with sugar and low in nutrients, will have them bouncing off the walls by mid-morning.

Several scientific studies suggest that children who eat breakfast do better at school, and children who are poorly nourished in general suffer more from not having a meal first thing in the day. It stands to reason that a child who is hungry and probably feeling wobbly due to low blood-sugar levels will find it hard to concentrate and learn, and be more likely to behave disruptively in class.

Think about it – if your child has not eaten for twelve hours or more, the fuel tanks are empty and need a fill-up of proteins, fats and carbohydrates, not just a quick fix of processed carbohydrates.

A protein breakfast is a vital weapon in your armoury against the symptoms we've just described. Protein is not only needed for children's growth and development – by adding it to their breakfast, it enhances the sustaining effect of the first meal of the day, keeping them going for longer, and making them less likely to demand or succumb to unhealthy sugary snacks mid-morning.

Breakfast needn't be conventional. Indeed, popular choices such as a bowl of breakfast cereal, or slices of white toast and marmalade, are far from ideal for children with developmental delay symptoms. They are high in processed starchy carbohydrates, and lack protein. Try the breakfasts in our meal plan. And, after the two weeks of the plan are over, don't rule out more 'unconventional' breakfasts, such as fishcakes, or a healthy sandwich. Breakfast is also a great time to add a portion or two of fruit to your child's intake.

Snacks

Healthy snacks are great for maintaining stable blood-sugar levels. They also help your child to hit their target of a minimum of five fruit and vegetable portions a day, and are an excellent opportunity to slip nuts and seeds into your child's diet.

Lunch

The weekday lunches in our 14-day plan are designed to be packed lunches, as this gives you maximum control over what your child eats.

However, you may prefer your child to have school dinners, for example if you'd rather not have to think about lunch and instead focus your energy on preparing healthy and interesting breakfasts and dinners. This is not a problem – you just need to be aware of the potential pitfalls. See if your child's school offers healthy school dinners – the rules governing school meals are getting a lot stricter, and it should certainly be possible for your child to choose food that fits in with the eating plan we recommend. Although you won't be able to use the lunches in the 14-day plan, you should be able to abide by the guidelines in Chapter 19. If your child is having school dinners, why not get a little more involved? Visit the school kitchen and chat to the staff. Ask to see the menu for the coming month or, as I did, invite yourself onto the school's Healthy Eating Committee.

If your child is old enough, explain what (and why) they should and should not choose, reinforcing the benefits of sticking to the plan. If your child is younger, you may need to enlist the assistance of the school-dinner helpers to ensure your child makes the right choices. Give them a list of things your child can and can't eat. If you explain why you are so concerned about your child's diet, you should almost certainly be able to get their help. If your child had a severe nut allergy or was diabetic you would certainly make sure they stuck to their diet, and that anyone providing food for them was aware of the situation.

Keeping track of what they eat

It's important for you to know whether your child has been able to follow the plan when they're not with you:

- If your child has a childminder or nanny, ask them to tell you what your child has eaten each day.
- If you give your child packed lunches, ask them to keep any leftovers in their lunchbox so you can see what they have eaten, and what they have left. This should also alert you if you've put in anything they can't stand!
- If your young child has school dinners, and you have been able to enlist the help of their canteen staff in helping your child follow the plan, you could ask the school-dinner helpers to make a quick note of how they are eating.

Dinner

Dinner can be problematic if your child is overexcited or tired (often they're overexcited *because* they're tired) and so less inclined to eat.

However, the healthy breakfasts, lunches and snacks in our 14-day plan should help sustain your child through the day, and make them less likely to be overly boisterous or cantankerous by suppertime. The dinners we recommend are hot and comforting, such as fish pie and rat stew (sorry, that's ratatouille!), and several are healthy versions of popular 'kid food', such as chicken burgers.

FAMILY MEALTIMES

Families who eat together, eat better. Research from Harvard Medical School showed that families which eat together are twice as likely to have five servings of fruit and vegetables a day as those who don't. A link was also found between eating family dinners and consuming less fried food and fizzy drinks. Also, the diets of the children who regularly ate family dinners were higher in many nutrients, including fibre, calcium, iron, folic acid and vitamins B6, B12, C and E.

According to a study of senior-school pupils in America, eating together brings benefits to mental wellbeing and performance at school. Researchers found that teenagers who regularly shared meals with their parents achieved higher academic scores and tended to be more satisfied with their lives and their future prospects.

Another American survey also found there was a decreased risk of unhealthy weight-control practices and substance abuse where families ate meals together.

Persuading children to eat healthily

It's been proven that the younger children are, the more adventurous they are when it comes to trying new foods – later they become more set in their ways. So make the most of their enthusiasm and receptiveness, by introducing as many different (healthy) tastes as you can.

Tasting tips:

- Make a 'one teaspoon taste' test rule. They have to taste just one teaspoon of any new foods, and if they like it they can have more.
- Don't make a big issue of the new food. Simply put a little of it on their plate, or produce it in a serving dish and say, 'I thought we'd all like to give this a try.'
- Children will often be prepared to try something if it is described as 'adult' food. Telling them it is the kind of thing adults like but perhaps they're not ready to eat it yet, often has them demanding to try it.
- Take your time with the introductions. One or perhaps two a week is enough.
- Introduce new foods at times when your child is likely to be hungriest – after school or at the evening meal.
- Arrange slices of favourite fruits on a large plate and include one new fruit. Serve the fruit platter as a snack with a natural yoghurt and honey dip, as an after-school snack, or as dessert after the evening meal.
- Offer your child a taste of foods you think may be an acquired taste, such as olives or avocados. Sometimes they will surprise you.
- Don't let your own personal tastes influence what you offer them. You may hate Brussels sprouts, but they could decide they're yummy.
- When they have friends round for a meal, introduce a new food. The chances are that if their friend likes it, then so will they!
- Avoid offering 'bribes' along the lines of 'You try these parsnips and then you can have a sweet.'

14-DAY EATING PLAN

We've designed the eating plan so it's tasty, and easy to prepare. Some of the meals and snacks are so simple they don't need a recipe. But where a recipe is needed, you'll find it at the back of this book.

DAY 1
Breakfast:
Scrambled egg on wholemeal toast
Slice of melon

Snack:
1 rice cake
A banana

Lunch:
A salad platter, suitable for a school packed lunch or at home (slices of cold chicken, carrot, cucumber, slices of pear, cherry tomatoes – try to introduce some sticks of celery and baby lettuce leaves)
2–3 breadsticks, preferably wholewheat

Snack:
A yoghurt pot filled with plain popcorn
A small glass of milk

Dinner:
Grilled fresh salmon fillet (see recipe) with steamed/boiled new potatoes, peas and sweet corn (or other vegetables if you prefer, as many as you like)
1 small natural yoghurt sweetened with 1tsp honey and some sultanas

DAY 2
Breakfast:
A bowl of porridge made with semi-skimmed milk, with (ideally) some blueberries mashed in – otherwise, try sweetening with 1tsp pure fruit spread or 1tsp 'good' drinking chocolate (no sweeteners)

Snack:
Handful of raisins

Lunch:
A wrap filled with hummus (see recipe) or low-fat cream cheese, with finely chopped red pepper and lettuce
Half a red pepper and 1 small carrot cut into strips
1 banana

Snack:
Handful of dried apricots, apple, pear or 2–3 breadsticks, ideally wholewheat
A small glass of milk

Dinner:
Grilled lamb chop with carrot rings, peas and mashed potato or boiled new potatoes

DAY 3
Breakfast:
A hard-boiled egg served with a wholemeal pitta bread cut into fingers (or wholemeal toast fingers)

Snack:
Any piece of fruit (with an oatcake if your child is hungry)

Lunch:
Lean-meat filled sandwich (turkey, chicken or ham) made with wholemeal bread
Small carton of natural yoghurt sweetened with 1tsp honey (optional) and topped with a few slices of banana, or mashed banana, or seasonal berries

Snack:
A finger of homemade fruity bar (see recipe)
A small glass of milk

Dinner:
Homemade lasagne (see recipe) with a salad made from lettuce and sliced tomato

DAY 4
Breakfast:
Quick omelette (see recipe), ideally with grilled tomatoes or mush-rooms, or sweet corn
1 banana and a sliced apple

Snack:
A piece of fruit (with an oatcake or two if your child is hungry)

Lunch:
Sandwich (preferably wholemeal bread) made with low-fat soft cheese
A small carton of veggie sticks – carrots, pepper, and cucumber
An orange or satsuma

Snack:
A finger of apricot and sultana slice (see recipe)
Small glass of milk

Dinner:
Baked chicken breast (see recipe) with a small baked jacket potato and a bowl of finger salad (carrot sticks, small lettuce leaves, cucumber slices)

DAY 5
Breakfast:
Baked beans on toast (preferably wholemeal)
A slice of melon

Snack:
A yoghurt pot of plain popcorn

Lunch:
Tinned salmon sandwich on wholemeal bread with chopped cucumber and low-fat mayonnaise (drain, and remove the skin from the salmon)
An apple

Snack:
2–3 breadsticks, preferably wholewheat, or vegetable sticks, with a little hummus (see recipe) or low-fat cream cheese for dipping
A small glass of milk

Dinner:
Home-made chicken and sweet-corn mini burgers (see recipe), served with brown rice (ideally, otherwise white rice) and a bowl of finger salad (carrot sticks, small lettuce leaves, cucumber slices)

DAY 6
Breakfast:
Wild West breakfast – grilled bacon with baked beans on wholemeal toast

Snack:
A handful of raisins or a piece of fruit

Lunch:
Slice of home-made ocean pizza (see recipe) served with a mixed salad
Pot of natural yoghurt with 1tsp honey (optional) or some raisins

Snack:
Home-made apricot and sultana slice (see recipe)
Small glass of milk

Dinner:
Fisherman's pie (see recipe) served with green beans or peas

DAY 7
Breakfast:
Bacon sarnie (preferably wholemeal) with grilled mushrooms or tomato
A slice of melon or mango slices

Snack:
A piece of fruit

Lunch:
Slice of leftover healthy home-made ocean pizza (see recipe)
A bowl of fruit topped with yoghurt

Snack:
A finger of fruity bar (see recipe)
A small glass of milk

Dinner:
Sunday roast dinner – chicken or lamb with roast potatoes and fresh vegetables
Fresh fruit salad topped with natural yoghurt and a drizzle of honey

DAY 8
Breakfast:
Bowl of fruit – for example a chopped banana, apple and half a mango – topped with a plain yoghurt, a drizzle of honey and 2tbsp no-sugar muesli and 1tbsp chopped nuts

Snack:
A piece of fruit (plus an oatcake if your child is still hungry)

Lunch:
Home-made chicken and sweet-corn mini burgers (see recipe) served with a salad platter of sticks of celery, carrot and cucumber, baby lettuce leaves, slices of pear or apple, and cherry tomatoes

Snack:
A small carton of yoghurt with half a mashed banana or some crushed berries stirred in

Dinner:
Rat stew (ratatouille, see recipe) poured over a grilled pork loin or grilled chicken breast, served with baby boiled potatoes

DAY 9
Breakfast:
A bowl of porridge made with semi-skimmed milk, with (ideally) some blueberries mashed in – otherwise, try sweetening with a 1tsp pure fruit spread or 1tsp 'good' drinking chocolate (no sweeteners)
A slice of melon

Snack:
A banana

Lunch:
Sliced roast chicken wrap with plenty of salad vegetables and low-fat mayonnaise
A pot of natural yoghurt with some chopped nuts and raisins stirred in
Piece of fruit

Snack:
An apple and a small piece of cheese
A glass of milk

Dinner:
Chilli con carne or chickpea chilli (see recipes), preferably with brown rice (otherwise white rice) and green beans or other vegetables

DAY 10
Breakfast:
Scrambled egg on wholemeal toast with grilled tomato
Piece of fruit

Snack:
A rice cake or an oatcake and a piece of fruit

Lunch:
A salmon-and-cucumber wholemeal sandwich (drain and remove skin from the salmon)
A small bowl of berry fruits topped with 2tbsp yoghurt

Snack:
A slice of apricot and sultana slice (see recipe)
A glass of milk

Dinner:
Home-made fish fingers and chunky chips (see recipes) with peas and/or sweet corn

DAY 11
Breakfast:
Cowboy eggs with tomato and sautéed potatoes (see recipe)

Snack:
A selection of vegetable sticks (celery, carrot, red pepper, cucumber) and an oatcake or two if your child is still hungry

Lunch:
A lean chicken or ham and salad wholemeal sandwich or wrap

Natural yoghurt with 'healthy' sweetening such as 1tsp honey, 1tsp 'good' hot chocolate powder (no sweeteners) or some raisins stirred in
A piece of fruit

Snack:
2 rice cakes spread with a little peanut butter or fruit spread
A small glass of milk

Dinner:
Baked chicken drumsticks with sweet-corn mash and peas or grilled tomatoes
A piece of fruit

DAY 12:
Breakfast:
Good quality low-fat chipolata sausages and baked beans on toast, preferably wholemeal

Snack:
A banana

Lunch:
Leftover chicken drumsticks with a salad platter of sticks of celery, carrot and cucumber, baby lettuce leaves, slices of pear or apple, cherry tomatoes
Pot of natural yoghurt with 1tsp honey or some nuts or raisins

Snack:
A yoghurt pot filled with plain popcorn
A glass of milk

Dinner:
Grilled salmon steak with rat stew (ratatouille) (see recipes)
A small natural fromage frais with plenty of berries, ideally fresh, or tinned in juice

DAY 13:
Breakfast:
French eggy toast with topping (see recipe) – choose from baked beans, bacon and chopped cooked tomatoes, or sliced (or mashed) banana (you could even try sliced banana and bacon!)

Snack:
A piece of fruit, plus an oatcake or two if your child is still hungry

Lunch:
Sardines on toast fingers with baby lettuce leaf boats filled with cottage cheese, and cherry tomatoes (see recipe)
A piece of fruit

Snack:
A slice of fruity bar (see recipe)
A small glass of milk

Dinner:
Chilli con carne (see recipe) with a little cheese grated on top, served with brown rice
Tinned fruit salad (in juice not syrup)

DAY 14:
Breakfast
Eggs in tomato baskets (see recipe)
A banana

Snack:
A piece of fruit, plus an oatcake or two if your child is still hungry

Lunch:
A sliced hard-boiled egg and cucumber sandwich with a bowl of salad vegetables and fruit (cherry tomatoes, cucumber slices, apple or pear slices)
Pot of natural yoghurt with some raisins

Snack:
2–3 wholewheat breadsticks with hummus dip (see recipe)

Dinner:
Baked fish with a breadcrumb and cheese topping (see recipe), served with new potatoes and fresh boiled vegetables

BENEFITS OF FOLLOWING THE EATING PLAN

- Stable energy levels throughout the day
- Ability to concentrate in school
- Better sleep
- Less likelihood of becoming unhealthily overweight
- Better health in the future – less risk of diseases such as type-2 diabetes, heart disease and cancer
- Healthier teeth
- A brain able to develop normally – not hampered by bad E numbers, trans fats and aspartame

These benefits are for *all* children, not just those with developmental delay.

17

THE EXERCISE, BRAIN EXERCISE AND DIET WORKBOOKS

THE EXERCISE WORKBOOK

This part of the book is to help you to plan out a healthy amount of activity for your child, and to chart their progress. You don't need to plan your child's life with military precision, and indeed a child who feels they are being 'organised' is likely to rebel.

Use these charts as a guideline, and copy the column headings and rows into an exercise book, or photocopy them on an enlarged setting.

Date (week beginning):...........................

	'Free' play or activity	'Organised' play or activity	Child's comments	Parents' comments
Monday				
Tuesday				
Wednesday				
Thursday				
Friday				
Saturday				
Sunday				

Total weekly activity target: Minimum 7 hours

Actual activity:...

How the charts work

Your child should have an average of at least an hour's physical activity each day. We've divided this into 'free' activity and 'organised' activity. For young children, free activity or play includes things like running around the garden, or playing in the playground. For a teenager it could include walking to school, or doing a paper round. Organised activity includes school PE lessons, sports club sessions, or organised family activities such as a family cycle ride.

There are spaces for you to fill in the activities your child takes part in, and for how long. For example, the first two columns for Monday might read: '½ hour playing in playground'; '¾ hour PE lesson'.

The 'Child's comments' column is for your child to fill in, or for you if your child is too young – ask them for their input, though. Perhaps your child might say they felt Saturday's bike ride was a bit tiring. But in a few weeks' time, it will hopefully be a breeze. Being able to track their improvement like this can be a great confidence builder for children.

In the 'Parents' comments' column you can make your own notes on how you think your child is progressing. Perhaps you tried a particular activity, but they didn't like it – you might like to make a note to yourself of something else that might work better. You can also make your own notes on how your child is progressing – your opinions may differ, and you might spot improvements they might not have noticed.

Try to get your child involved. If you transfer the charts into an exercise book, they might like to decorate it with drawings, stickers or pictures cut out of magazines.

THE BRAIN EXERCISE WORKBOOK

If your child is doing the brain exercises (both the 'general' brain exercises, and those targeting the left or right side of the brain), you'll probably want to track their progress.

As with the physical exercises, we've provided a chart for you to copy into an exercise book, or photocopy on an enlarged setting – write the exercises your child is doing in the 'exercises' column. If your child is old enough, try to get them involved.

Date (week beginning):.........................

	'General' brain exercises	Right- or left-side brain exercises	Child's comments	Parents' comments
Monday				
Tuesday				
Wednesday				
Thursday				
Friday				
Saturday				
Sunday				

THE DIET WORKBOOK

After completing the 14-day eating plan (see chapter 16), you should begin to see improvements in your child's symptoms and behaviour, particularly if they were previously eating a diet low in important nutrients such as vitamins and minerals, and high in sugar, salt, bad fats and chemical additives.

But eating healthily is not a 'cure' – you can't go back to your child's old eating ways and expect the benefits to continue, or even to last. It's got to be a changed way of life.

However, it's not practical to repeat the 14-day plan, over and over, for ever. Not only would you and your child get horribly bored, you also wouldn't be able to vary their diet to include the widest variety of different foods (within healthy limits, of course). And the more varied a child's diet is, the greater their chances of hitting their targets for all the different nutrients, vitamins, minerals, phytochemicals and the like. So for that reason, we've prepared this chapter of advice on adapting the principles of the plan for the way ahead.

The way ahead

Memory jogger
You need to:

- Dump the junk
- Up the essential fatty acids
- Consider providing vitamins and minerals
- Cut the sugar

A good, basic plan for a healthy balanced diet for a child would include the list below, but you might need to adapt it, according to your child's age and appetite. For example, a teenager might need up to ten portions of starchy carbohydrates every day, while a small child might need slightly smaller portions of protein foods, such as meat, chicken, fish and dairy products.

In general:

- Eat moderate amounts of fats – but good fats only
- Have minimal amounts of added sugar
- Add omega essential fatty acid supplements

To keep fat intake 'sensible', avoid deep-frying foods, use the healthy fats we recommend in this book, and use only a thin scraping of a healthy spread on bread.

Daily:

- From 5 portions of starchy carbohydrates, preferably whole-meal – increase the number according to your child's age and appetite, up to 12 portions for hungry teenage boys
- At least 3 portions of fruit
- At least 3 portions of vegetables
- 3 child-sized portions of meat, fish, eggs or pulses
- 3 portions of dairy foods (2 portions for children aged 3–8)

Weekly:

- Fish minimum of three times a week
- Aim for two portions of oily fish a week
- Red meat maximum twice a week (because it is high in saturated fat)
- Crisps maximum of once a week, and only 'plain' ready-salted varieties (to minimise additives)
- One *small* bar chocolate (good-quality chocolate only)

If your child can do without crisps and chocolate, then all the better. But we believe it's better to allow them a small amount every week, if that is what it takes to keep them on the healthy eating plan.

Banned foods:

We don't like to ban foods – most foods are allowable in moderation, or as an occasional treat. But the following foods really have *no* place in your child's diet:

- Fizzy drinks
- Fruit squash
- Luridly coloured, additive-packed sweets

What is a portion?

Here are some examples.

Starchy carbohydrates:

- 1 slice bread
- 1 egg-sized potato
- 2 heaped tbsp cooked rice or pasta

Fruit:

- An apple, orange, peach or nectarine
- A small banana
- 10–12 grapes
- 2 mandarins, clementines or satsumas
- 2 kiwi fruit or dessert plums

- A slice of melon or pineapple
- 7 strawberries
- 2–3 tbsp drained tinned fruit (in juice, not syrup)
- A small (150ml) glass of pure fruit juice (diluted with water)
- 1 tbsp raisins or sultanas
- 3 ready-to-eat dried unsulphured apricots, or 2 dried figs

Vegetables:

- 1 medium salad
- 3 tbsp cooked vegetables
- 2 small raw carrots

Protein foods:
- 1 egg
- 45g lean meat, poultry or fish
- 2 tbsp cooked beans (such as red kidney beans or baked beans)
- 1 tbsp nuts or seeds

Adult-sized portions of protein foods are generally accepted to be twice these amounts.

Dairy foods:

- 200ml glass of semi-skimmed or skimmed milk
- 150g pot of low-fat yoghurt
- A matchbox sized (30g) piece of cheese

Healthy breakfast tips
Try to eat breakfast with your children. If they see you think it is an important enough meal for you to have every day, they will think the same.

- Set the table and get everything ready the night before to save time in the morning. As children get older this is an easy task they can take over.
- Try to avoid breakfast being a last-minute affair. Encourage your child to get everything ready for school before they go to bed so they're not rushing around looking for missing PE

kit, lost homework and the like when they should be eating breakfast.

- Use wholemeal bread, and make a rule that toast must have 'topping' (e.g. healthy beans, or sardines) rather than just being spread with jam or marmalade.
- Try to include a piece of fruit with breakfast, or a small glass of diluted fruit juice.

Some ideas for fillings for sandwiches and wraps

- Sliced roast chicken, with crispy lettuce and pepper strips
- Sliced poached chicken breast, low-fat mayonnaise and finely chopped salad vegetables
- Cooked sliced chicken with salad vegetables and pickle
- Canned salmon (drain, and remove the skin), mashed with a teaspoon of low-fat salad cream, with slices of cucumber
- Tinned tuna with finely chopped cucumber, and lettuce
- Tinned tuna, sweet corn, a tiny bit of low-fat salad cream and freshly ground black pepper
- Low-fat soft cheese, lean ham and sliced tomato
- Sliced hard-boiled egg with lettuce and tomato slices
- Chopped hard-boiled egg, cress and low-fat mayonnaise or salad cream
- Low-fat soft cheese with grated carrot or finely sliced dried apricot
- Low-fat soft cheese, tomato, cucumber and lettuce
- Peanut butter (not too much!) and sliced or mashed banana

The eating plan workbook

This part of the book is to help you map out a healthy eating plan for your child, and monitor their progress. Use this chart as a guideline, and copy the column headings and rows into an exercise book, or photocopy them on an enlarged setting.

You can plan out a week's menus in advance, filling in the meals and snacks for each day. There are also sections for you to fill in the number of portions of food groups (such as protein, starchy carbohydrates, fruit, vegetables, etc.), so you can aim for the number of portions listed on pages 196–7. The final column is for comments – from you and your child – on things like foods your child particularly did or didn't like, and any improvements in their behaviour and other symptoms.

	Breakfast	Snack	Lunch	Snack	Dinner	Starchy carbs (5–11 portions)	Protein foods (3 portions)	Fruit (3 portions or more)	Vegetables (5 portions or more)	Dairy (3 portions)	COMMENTS
Monday											
Tuesday											
Wednesday											
Thursday											
Friday											
Saturday											
Sunday											

Do your best to meet the targets each day, but don't worry too much if you don't hit them every time. It's the average that matters – in general, if a child doesn't eat enough vegetables (for example) on one day, they can make it up later. Your child's diet is very important, but you have better things to do with your time than get stressed about whether they have had one too many starchy carbohydrate portions, or one too few pieces of fruit on a particular day.

18

THE 14-DAY PLAN RECIPES

BREAKFASTS

Quick Omelette
Serves 1

1 large egg
1 tbsp milk
1 tsp chopped fresh parsley, optional
Salt and pepper

1. Beat the egg with the milk in a bowl, with the parsley (if used). Lightly wipe a small nonstick frying pan with olive oil and heat gently. Add the egg mixture and cook until the bottom of the omelette is lightly browned and the top is beginning to set. Fold the omelette in half. Cook for a further minute.
2. Serve, ideally, with grilled tomatoes, mushrooms or sweet corn.

Cowboy eggs with tomato and sautéed potatoes
Serves 4

4 eggs
200g cold cooked new potatoes, diced
1 can chopped tomato

Freshly ground black pepper
1 tbsp olive oil

1. Heat the olive oil in a large frying pan. Fry the potatoes until they are browned.
2. Tip the chopped tomato over the potatoes in the pan and bring to the boil. Break an egg into a small bowl and slip into the pan. Repeat one at a time with the other eggs. Cook until the eggs are set.
3. Serve each egg with a portion of the tomatoes and potatoes.

Note: if you like, you can remove the potatoes before step 2, keep them warm, then pour the tomatoes and egg over them when you're ready to serve. The potatoes stay crispier this way.

French eggy toast with topping
Serves 1

1 egg
1 slice bread, preferably wholemeal
A little olive oil, for the pan

1. Break the egg onto a plate, and beat well with a fork. Dip the bread into the egg so that both sides are well coated. Gently heat a nonstick frying pan and wipe with a little olive oil.
2. Place the egg-soaked bread into the pan and fry on both sides until golden brown. Transfer to a plate and add your chosen topping.

Toppings: Choose from baked beans, bacon and chopped cooked tomatoes, or sliced (or mashed) banana. You could even try sliced banana and bacon.

Eggs in tomato baskets
Serves 1

1 egg
1 firm medium-sized tomato

Freshly ground black pepper
1 slice bread, preferably wholemeal

1. Preheat the oven to 180C/Gas 4.
2. Break the egg into a small bowl. Slice the top off the tomato and remove the seeds using a teaspoon, taking care not to damage the outer shell of the tomato. Place on a nonstick baking tray and pour the egg into the hollowed-out tomato. Season with a little ground black pepper. Bake in the oven for 15 minutes or until the white of the egg is set. (If you like you can cook the cut-off top of the tomato for the last 5 minutes of cooking time and then pop it back on top of the tomato before serving.)
3. Serve on a slice of toast, spread with a little healthy spread.

LUNCHES

Ocean pizza
Serves 4

1 large pizza base
1 small tin chopped tomatoes
½tsp dried mixed herbs or oregano
3tbsp sweet corn
3 medium-sized tomatoes
1 small onion, cut into rings
6 mushrooms, sliced
2 cans sardines in olive oil, drained
Grated cheese
Freshly ground black pepper
Handful of fresh basil leaves (optional)

1. Preheat the oven to 200C/Gas 6.
2. Put the tinned chopped tomato into a saucepan with the herbs. Boil gently for about 10 minutes until the liquid has evaporated and you have a thick sauce. Allow to cool.
3. Spread the sauce over the pizza base. Then arrange the tomatoes, mushrooms and onions over the sauce on the

base. Sprinkle over the sweet corn. Drain the sardines and arrange on the base like the spokes of a wheel. Sprinkle over the grated cheese. Season with black pepper. Tear the basil leaves, if using, and sprinkle over the pizza.

4. Bake in the centre of the oven for 15–20 minutes until the base is crisp and the cheese is melted and golden. Serve with a large salad.

Note: If you prefer, you can use tinned mackerel or tuna instead of sardines.

Sardines on toast
Serves 2

1 tin of sardines or mackerel in oil
2 slices of bread, preferably wholemeal
1 'little gem' lettuce
4 cherry tomatoes
1 small carton cottage cheese (plain or with pineapple)
Home-made tomato sauce (see page 223) for dipping

1. Drain the fish and mash. Toast the bread and spread the mashed fish on each slice. Grill until the fish is heated – watch carefully to see it does not burn. Cut into fingers.
2. Wash and separate the lettuce leaves and spoon a little cottage cheese into each leaf so it resembles a boat. Arrange the toast fingers, the lettuce leaf boats and cherry tomatoes on plates. Serve with a little home-made tomato sauce to dip the toast fingers into.

DINNERS

Pan-fried or grilled fresh salmon
Serves 4

4 salmon fillets, skin removed
Freshly ground black pepper

1. Season the salmon fillet with freshly ground black pepper. Place the salmon in a nonstick frying pan (no need to add oil – there is plenty in the fish). Gently pan-fry the fish until it is cooked, turning once. It will only need a few minutes' cooking time on each side.
2. If you'd prefer to grill the salmon, cook it for 4–6 minutes each side, depending on the thickness of the fillet (thick pieces will take longer).

Serve with boiled new potatoes and vegetables.

Note: If you want a tasty sauce to serve alongside the salmon, combine a tablespoon of home-made tomato sauce (see page 223) with a tablespoon of good-quality low-fat mayonnaise in a small ramekin. Children like the taste and the lovely pink colour.

Home-made lasagne
Serves 4

For the meat sauce:
350g lean minced beef
1 large onion finely chopped
1 large carrot, finely chopped
2 sticks celery, finely chopped
1 clove garlic, crushed
1 large can chopped tomatoes
2tbsp tomato purée
100ml beef stock made with a stock cube
½tsp dried mixed herbs or oregano
Salt and freshly ground black pepper
Some no-need-to-pre-cook lasagne sheets (depending on the size of your dish)
3 medium tomatoes, sliced

For the cheese sauce:
300ml semi-skimmed milk
3tbsp cornflour
3tbsp water
50g grated mature Cheddar cheese
Freshly ground black pepper

1. Preheat the oven to 190C/Gas 5.
2. Place the meat in a large saucepan and fry gently with the onion, garlic, carrot and celery for 10 minutes until the vegetables are tender and the meat is no longer pink. Stir from time to time. Drain off any excess fat. Add all of the remaining ingredients for the meat sauce, except the sliced tomato, and stir. Season with salt and pepper. Simmer gently for 30 minutes.
3. Take a large ovenproof dish and cover the bottom with the cooked meat sauce, then a layer of lasagne sheets. Continue to layer the meat and lasagne, finishing with a lasagne layer. Top with the sliced tomato.
4. To make the cheese sauce: In a small bowl blend the cornflour and water. Place the milk in a saucepan and bring to a simmer. Add the cornflour mixture and stir in the cheese. Cook gently for 2 minutes until the sauce has thickened and the cheese melted. Season with pepper. Pour the sauce over the lasagne. Bake in the oven for 30–35 minutes.

Baked chicken breast
Serves 4

4 small chicken breasts, skin removed
Freshly ground black pepper

1. Preheat the oven to 180C/Gas 4.
2. Place the chicken breasts on a large piece of baking foil and sprinkle with black pepper. Wrap into a loose parcel and bake in the oven for 25–30 minutes or until the chicken is properly cooked. Cut each breast into 4 or 5 slices and arrange on a plate.

If you want chicken as a 'Sunday roast' but don't want to cook a whole chicken, this a great way to cook it. Simply slice the cooked chicken thinly and arrange on a serving plate.

Chicken and sweet-corn mini burgers
Serves 4 (Makes 16 mini burgers – use 8 and freeze the remaining 8 for later)

500g chicken, minced
1 medium onion, peeled and very finely chopped
1tsp oil
1 small can sweet corn
1 medium carrot, grated
2tbsp tomato purée
Freshly ground black pepper
2tbsp fresh parsley, finely chopped (optional)

1. Put all the ingredients into a bowl and mix together thoroughly. Form into 16 burgers.
2. Wipe a nonstick pan with olive oil and gently fry the mini burgers for 5–7 minutes on each side until they are golden and completely cooked through.
3. Serve with a portion of rice or chunky chips (see page 210) and a finger salad.

Fisherman's pie
Serves 4

500g potatoes
450g white-fish fillets
300ml semi-skimmed milk
75g mature Cheddar cheese, grated
200g frozen mixed vegetables
8 cherry tomatoes, halved
2tbsp fresh parsley, chopped
3tbsp plain flour
Salt and pepper

1. Preheat the oven to 180C/Gas 4.
2. Boil the potatoes until tender, drain and mash with 25g of the cheese.
3. Put the frozen vegetables into a saucepan with the tomatoes, fish and milk and simmer gently for 6–8 minutes until they

are cooked. Turn off the heat and lift the vegetables and the fish from the saucepan, keeping the milk to make the sauce. Place the vegetables and the fish into a large ovenproof dish.

4. To make the sauce: Put the flour into a bowl and add enough water to make a thin paste. Pour the paste into the milk and beat well. Bring the milk to the boil, stirring all the time. Add the remaining cheese and simmer for 2 minutes until the sauce has thickened and the cheese melted. Add the parsley. Season with salt and pepper. Pour over the fish and vegetables in the ovenproof dish. Top with the cheesy mashed potato.

5. Bake for 20 minutes or until piping hot.

'Rat' stew
Serves 4

1 onion, halved and sliced
1 clove garlic, crushed
1 red pepper, de-seeded and sliced into thin strips
1 medium courgette, sliced
½ aubergine, cubed (optional)
4 ripe tomatoes
6 medium mushrooms, quartered
2tbsp tomato purée
150ml water
½tsp dried mixed herbs
½tsp sugar
Salt and pepper
1tbsp olive oil

1. Place the oil in a large saucepan and gently fry the onion and garlic for 2 minutes. Add the remaining vegetables and cook, stirring for 2 minutes.

2. Add the water, tomato purée, mixed herbs and sugar. Season with salt and pepper. Bring to the boil, cover the pan and reduce the heat. Simmer for 15–20 minutes until the vegetables are tender.

3. Serve the ratatouille with a grilled pork loin chop or baked chicken breast, and boiled baby new potatoes.

Chilli con carne
Serves 4

225g extra-lean minced beef
1 medium onion, finely chopped
1 clove garlic, crushed
½tsp chilli powder
1tsp mixed herbs
1tbsp tomato purée
1 large can chopped tomatoes
1 large can red kidney beans, drained and rinsed
Salt and freshly ground black pepper

1. Put the onion, minced beef and garlic into a large saucepan. Fry for about 5 minutes, stirring all the time until the meat is no longer pink. Drain off any excess fat.
2. Add the chilli powder, mixed herbs, tomato purée and chopped tomatoes. Stir together. Season with salt and pepper.
3. Simmer gently for 30 minutes, stirring occasionally. Add a little water if necessary. Add the drained kidney beans and simmer gently for another 10 minutes.
4. Serve with rice (preferably brown) and fresh vegetables.

Chickpea chilli
Serves 4

1 large plus 1 small can of chickpeas, rinsed and drained
1 medium onion, chopped
1 small clove garlic, crushed
1 large can tomatoes
½tsp sugar
150ml vegetable stock
¼tsp chilli powder (or to taste)
1 carrot, grated or finely chopped
12 cauliflower or broccoli florets
1 red pepper, de-seeded and chopped
2tbsp low-fat natural yoghurt (optional)
Salt and pepper

1. Lightly oil a saucepan and gently fry the onion for 5–6 minutes until golden. Add the garlic and spices and cook for a further minute.
2. Add the stock and sugar. Add the chickpeas, canned tomatoes, red pepper and cauliflower or broccoli. Simmer until the vegetables are tender (about 10 minutes). Just before serving, stir in the yoghurt, if using.
3. Serve with rice (preferably brown) and a green salad or fresh boiled vegetables.

Home-made fish fingers
Serves 1

150g white-fish fillet
1 egg, beaten
2 slices bread, preferably wholemeal, crumbed
Freshly ground black pepper
Pinch of salt

1. Preheat the oven to 200C/Gas 6.
2. Cut the fish fillets into 2.5cm (1-inch) wide strips. Beat the egg on a flat plate and put the breadcrumbs, a pinch of salt and ground black pepper on another plate. Dip the fish fingers into the egg and then into the breadcrumbs to coat thoroughly.
3. Place the fish fingers on a baking tray and spray lightly with a spray olive oil. Bake the fingers for 10 minutes. Turn them over and cook for another 10–15 minutes (depending on the thickness of the fish) until the crumb is golden and fish is cooked through. If they brown too quickly, turn down the oven heat.

Chunky chips
Serves 4

4 large potatoes
1 tbsp oil
Freshly ground pepper, if liked

1. Preheat oven to 220C/Gas 7.

2. Wash the potatoes but don't peel them. Boil the potatoes whole for 5 minutes, then drain and cool immediately under cold water. Cut into thick chips. Place the oil in a bowl and add the chips. Toss to lightly coat them in the oil.
3. Lay the chips on a nonstick baking tray or a piece of non-stick baking paper. Bake for 25–35 minutes until they are cooked and golden. Turn a couple of times during cooking so the chips brown evenly. If they brown too quickly, turn the oven heat down a little.

Chicken dippers with tomato dip
Serves 4

4 small chicken breasts, skin removed
40g Parmesan, finely grated (optional)
100g fine dry breadcrumbs (home-made)
1 large egg
Freshly ground black pepper

1. Preheat the oven to 180C/Gas 4.
2. Cut the chicken breasts into 2.5cm (1-inch) wide strips. Beat the egg on a flat plate and put the breadcrumbs and ground black pepper (combined with the grated Parmesan, if using) on another plate. Dip the chicken strips into the egg and then into the breadcrumbs to coat thoroughly.
3. Place the chicken strips on a baking tray and spray lightly with a spray olive oil. Bake the chicken dippers for 10 minutes. Turn the dippers over and cook for another 10–15 minutes until the crumb is golden and chicken is cooked through. Serve with a little fresh tomato sauce (see page 223).

Tattie wedges
Serves 4

4 large potatoes, washed but not peeled
Ground black pepper/Cajun spice/sweet paprika
1tbsp olive oil

1. Preheat the oven to 220C/Gas 7.

2. Wash the potatoes but leave the skins on. Cut each potato into quarters lengthways. Then cut each of the quarters into thick wedges. Put the oil and any seasoning you want to use into a large bowl and add the potatoes. Toss them to get all of the surfaces lightly coated with oil – it's easier to use your hands, but a little bit messy!

3. Lay the wedges on a nonstick baking tray or nonstick baking paper. Bake for 25–35 minutes or until the potatoes are tender. Turn the wedges a couple of times during the cooking time so they brown evenly.

Baked fish with breadcrumb and cheese topping
Serves 4

4 fillets of fresh white fish such as cod (or use frozen and defrost thoroughly)
2 slices wholemeal (or good-quality white) bread
2tbsp grated Cheddar cheese
Freshly ground black pepper
1tbsp parsley (optional)
1tbsp olive oil

1. Preheat the oven to 180C/Gas 4.
2. Place the fillets on a nonstick baking tray. Make the bread into crumbs and place in a small bowl. Add all the other ingredients to the bowl and mix together.
3. Press onto the top of the fillets and bake in the oven for 12–15 minutes or until the fish is cooked through (this will depend on the thickness of the fish) and the topping is crisp.
4. Serve with mashed potatoes and a selection of vegetables or a green salad.

SNACKS AND MISCELLANEOUS:

Healthy hummus
Serves 4
1 large can of chickpeas
1 small clove garlic, crushed

1tbsp olive oil
1tbsp lemon juice
3tbsp natural low-fat yoghurt
Salt and freshly ground black pepper

1. Place all the ingredients, except the salt and pepper, in a blender and whiz until smooth. Taste and adjust the seasoning by adding a little salt and pepper if needed.
2. Cover and chill in the fridge. Serve in a wrap or pitta bread, with crackers, or on toast fingers.

Fruity bar
Makes approx 12 pieces

85g olive spread (suitable for baking)
3tbsp set honey
50g demerara sugar
2tbsp milk
150g porridge oats
½tsp mixed spice
80g sultanas
50g walnuts or pecans, chopped
80g no-need-to-soak apricots
25g desiccated coconut
75g seeds (any combination of pumpkin, sesame, sunflower)

1. Preheat the oven to 190C/Gas 5 and lightly grease an 18cm×18cm square baking tin.
2. Place the honey, olive spread and sugar in a saucepan and cook over a gentle heat for 5 minutes, stirring all the time, until it resembles a thick sauce. Add all the remaining ingredients and mix together well.
3. Transfer the mixture into a greased baking tin and bake in the middle of the oven for 25–30 minutes until golden brown and firm. Remove from the oven and mark into fingers. Leave in the tin to cool completely before cutting along the marks. Store in a lidded container.

Apricot and sultana slice
Makes approximately 12 pieces

100g no-need-to-soak apricots, chopped
50g sultanas
75g wholemeal self-raising flour
75g porridge oats (not instant oats)
25g soft light-brown sugar
100g butter or low-fat spread (suitable for baking)
1tbsp golden syrup
Juice of 1 orange

1. Preheat the oven to 180C/Gas 4 and lightly grease an 18cm×18cm square baking tin.
2. Place the apricots, sultanas and orange juice in a small saucepan and cook gently until the juice has been absorbed. Leave to cool.
3. Combine the dry ingredients in a large bowl. Place the sugar, syrup and butter or low-fat spread in a saucepan and heat until the fat has melted. Pour onto the oat mixture and mix thoroughly.
4. Put two-thirds of the oat mixture into the baking tin and press down evenly. Spoon the apricot and sultana mixture over the top. Then put the rest of the oat mixture on top. It doesn't matter if there are gaps where the apricot and sultana mixture shows through.
5. Bake in the middle of the oven for 25–30 minutes until golden brown. Remove from the oven and mark into fingers. Leave in the tin to cool completely before cutting along the marks, or the slices may crumble. Store in a lidded container.

19

MORE RECIPES

Here are some more healthy recipes to add to your cooking repertoire.

Croque Monsieur
A tasty breakfast or simple lunch
Serves 4

8 slices of bread
5 lean slices cooked ham
4 thin slices of half-fat Cheddar cheese
Ground black pepper

1. Preheat the grill. Toast 4 slices of bread on both sides and 4 slices of bread on one side.
2. Butter one side of the bread that has been toasted on both sides. Top with the ham and cheese. Season with black pepper. Lay the remaining slices of bread on the sandwich with the untoasted side upwards.
3. Grill the untoasted side of the sandwich. Cut each sandwich into two triangles and served with a grilled tomato or mushrooms.

Sticky lamb steaks
Serves 4

4 lamb steaks, fat removed
4 sprigs rosemary
3tbsp redcurrant jelly
2tbsp malt vinegar
Ground black pepper

1. Strip the leaves from the rosemary and finely chop.
2. Warm the redcurrant jelly and the vinegar in a small saucepan until the jelly has melted, and add the rosemary.
3. Brush the lamb steaks with a little of the redcurrant sauce and grill for 4 minutes. Turn the lamb steaks over and brush with the sauce. Grill for another 4 minutes. Turn over again and brush with the sauce, cook for a further minute, turn over and brush the other side with sauce and cook for a further minute.
4. Place the lamb steaks on serving plates and pour over any remaining sauce.
5. Serve with boiled or mashed potatoes and peas, or a mixed salad.

Basic tomato pasta sauce
Ring the changes by adding different vegetables, fish or chicken
Serves 4

1tsp olive oil
1 medium onion, finely chopped
1 can chopped tomatoes
1tbsp tomato purée
1 large clove garlic, finely chopped (optional)
1tsp sugar
Freshly ground black pepper

1. Put the olive oil into a large saucepan and gently fry the onions and garlic until softened but not coloured.

2. Add the other ingredients, and stir to combine. Place a lid on the saucepan and simmer the sauce gently for 15 minutes.

Variations
Add any of these to the sauce when you are cooking it, or think of your own veggie additions – it's a great way of getting children to eat their vegetables:

- Broccoli and sweet corn
- Diced peppers and courgette
- Peas and diced carrots
- French beans, spinach, spring onions and courgette

This basic tomato sauce can also be used as a basc for stews, casseroles and baked savoury dishes, or as a base for mince dishes.

You can also add flaked tinned salmon, mackerel or tuna and heat until piping hot before pouring over pasta. Or try adding chopped cooked chicken, lean ham or chopped cooked turkey.

A tasty bake can be made by cooking chicken breasts (skin removed) in a frying pan for 3 minutes on each side and transferring to an ovenproof dish. Pour over the basic tomato sauce. Top with some fresh brown breadcrumbs combined with two tablespoons of grated cheese. Bake in the oven on 180C/Gas 4 for 30 minutes or until the chicken is completely cooked through. Serve with mashed potato and fresh green vegetables or some pasta and a salad. Remember when making pasta dishes – heavy on the vegetables, easy on the pasta.

Tip
When you have some spare time make a large batch of the tomato sauce and freeze in meal-size portions, so all you have to do is take a portion out of the freezer and put it into the fridge the evening before you need it. It will be defrosted and ready to use by the next day.

Mini meatballs
These are ideal to serve for lunch in pitta bread pockets with salad or for supper with pasta
Makes 20

250g lean minced beef
1 small onion finely chopped
100g frozen mixed vegetables, cooked and drained
2tbsp homemade tomato table sauce or 1tbsp tomato purée mixed
with 1tbsp water.
Freshly ground black pepper

1. Preheat the oven to 180C/Gas 4.
2. Place the frozen mixed vegetables in a saucepan with water
   and cook as instructed on the packet. Drain and mash the
   vegetables. Allow them to get cold.
3. Place the minced beef in a bowl with the mashed vegetables
   and the tomato sauce or purée, and mix well. Break into 24
   even-sized pieces and form into balls. Place the balls on a
   baking sheet and bake in the oven for 12–15 minutes until
   the meatballs are cooked.
4. Cool completely and freeze any you do not need to use at
   the present time.

To make the stuffed pittas, split the pitta and fill with salad – lettuce,
sliced tomato, cucumber, onion rings – along with 4 mini meatballs.
Drizzle a little home-made tomato 'ketchup' into the pockets. To
use with a basic tomato sauce, add the required number of meatballs
to the sauce and heat until the meatballs are piping hot.

Tuna (or salmon) and bean salad
Serves 4

1 large can salmon or tuna skinned, drained and flaked
1 small can sweet corn
1 small onion, finely chopped
1 tin kidney beans, washed and drained
1 red pepper, de-seeded and chopped
3 tomatoes, cut into wedges
4 large handfuls of shredded lettuce
2tsp olive oil
2tsp vinegar

1. Combine all the ingredients in a bowl and toss lightly. Arrange on a plate and drizzle over the oil and vinegar.
2. Serve with a warmed crusty wholemeal roll or potato wedges.

Stir-fried chicken and vegetables
Serves 4

3 chicken breasts, thinly sliced
1tsp Chinese 5-Spice powder
1 clove garlic, peeled and chopped
2tbsp cornflour
1tsp vegetable oil
300g bag of ready-prepared stir-fry vegetables
2 pineapple rings canned in fruit juice not syrup (reserve 2tbsp of the juice)
1tbsp vinegar
2tsp soy sauce
2tbsp water
Noodles or rice, to serve

1. Place the Chinese 5-Spice powder, garlic and 1tbsp of the cornflour in a bowl. Add the chicken and toss together.
2. Heat the oil in a large nonstick frying pan or wok and stir-fry the chicken for 4–5 minutes until cooked, stirring all the time. Remove the chicken from the pan and keep warm.
3. Add the vegetables to the wok and stir-fry for another 2–3 minutes.
4. Add the pineapple and the cooked chicken to the pan. Combine the pineapple juice, vinegar, soy sauce, water and remaining tablespoon of cornflour in a small bowl and add to the pan. Cook, stirring, until the sauce has thickened, the vegetables are lightly cooked and the chicken is piping hot.
5. Serve with the noodles or rice (preferably brown).

Note: Make sure your Chinese 5-Spice powder contains just spices and no additives.

Texas burgers
Serves 4

350g lean beef mince
40g fresh white breadcrumbs
1 small onion, finely chopped
1 medium egg, beaten
Freshly ground black pepper

Optional (add any one of the following to the mixture):
1tsp mild mustard
1tsp creamed horseradish sauce
1tbsp home-made tomato 'ketchup' (see page 223)
1tsp Worcestershire sauce
1 clove garlic, crushed

1. Place the beef and breadcrumbs into a bowl. Gently fry the onion in a lightly oiled pan for a couple of minutes until it has softened. Transfer to the bowl. Add freshly ground black pepper and one of the optional extras if you like. Add the egg to the bowl and, using your hands, mix the ingredients together thoroughly.
2. Form into 4 to 6 thick burgers. Place on a plate and refrigerate for an hour to allow the burgers to become firm.
3. Cook the burgers in a dry pan on a gentle heat for 6–8 minutes on each side until they are cooked through. You can also cook them on a moderate grill for a similar time.
4. Serve with a wholemeal bap, sweet-corn relish or salsa, and a green salad.

Sleepy sausages in blankets
Serves 4

4 good-quality sausages
1 medium onion, finely sliced
4 soft tortillas
2 tomatoes, chopped
2tsp home-made tomato 'ketchup' (see page 223)
A little low-fat olive spray

1. Preheat the oven to 180C/Gas 4.
2. Grill the sausages. Cut each of the cooked sausages in half, lengthways. Gently fry the onion until it is golden and caramelised. Add the chopped tomatoes and cook for 2 minutes.
3. Place some of the onion and tomato sauce in a line down the centre of each of the wraps, and add two halves of sausage. Roll up the wrap and place on a nonstick baking tray and spray with a little olive oil. Cook for 8–10 minutes or until the wraps are crisp.
4. Serve with a large salad.

Gravy, sauces and relishes

Gravy

You can make a tasty gravy to serve with meat, without resorting to instant gravy mixes, many of which may contain additives, colourings and sweeteners. It needn't be a challenge – it's all in the stock. If you either make your own stock using meat bones, or buy a good organic beef, vegetable or chicken stock and then thicken it with cornflour, you'll have a delicious gravy. For even more flavour you can add some onion purée – keep some in the freezer.

To make a vegetable gravy:

Use half a litre of well-flavoured vegetable stock (home-made, see below, or use a good-quality organic stock or bouillon powder with no nasty additives). Heat in a saucepan. Combine 1tbsp (heaped) cornflour with 2tbsp cold water to form a paste. Add to the stock and bring to the boil until the gravy thickens slightly. Season with freshly ground black pepper.

Meat gravy

Use bought organic beef stock (check there are no nasty ingredients) to make a gravy to accompany red meat, or good organic chicken stock for a gravy to accompany chicken dishes.

Concentrated vegetable stock

600ml water
1 sage leaf
6 peppercorns

2 sprigs fresh thyme
Large sprig fresh parsley
1 medium carrot, scrubbed and finely chopped
1 stick celery, roughly chopped
1 medium onion, chopped
1 small leek, chopped (optional)
1 small turnip or piece of swede, roughly chopped
Pinch of salt

1. Place all the ingredients in a saucepan, cover and simmer for 1¼ hours. During the cooking, top up with water so the vegetables are always covered.
2. Strain the stock and discard the herbs and vegetables, cool the stock, and store in the fridge for up to 3 days, or freeze in 150ml containers.

To make onion purée to add to gravy
Chop 3 onions. Place in a saucepan and cover with water. Simmer gently for 15 minutes, adding a little more water if necessary. Allow to cool slightly and tip into a blender. Whiz until the onion is smooth. Pour into ice-cube trays and freeze. Add 2 or 3 cubes to a gravy for extra flavour (you can add them frozen and then reheat the gravy).

Red pepper, sweet corn and coriander relish
A quick relish to serve with grilled or baked chicken or chicken burgers
Serves 4

2 medium red peppers
1 small mild fresh red chilli
2 spring onions
Handful of fresh coriander leaves
1tbsp olive oil

1. De-seed and roughly chop the red peppers, the chilli, and the spring onions. Gently fry in the oil for 10 minutes until softened.
2. Transfer into a food processor or blender and whiz for a few seconds. Add the coriander leaves and whiz for a few more seconds (you don't want it to turn into a paste).

3. Spoon the relish into a bowl and chill until needed.

Home-made tomato ketchup
Tomato sauce is simple to make, tastes delicious, and is much healthier than bought ketchup. Try these recipes:

Home-made tomato 'ketchup' – 1
1tbsp olive oil
150g onion, finely chopped
450g tomatoes (preferably plum or beef tomatoes), skins and seeds removed and chopped
3 small sticks celery, finely chopped
2 cloves garlic, crushed
225ml water
¼tsp salt
2tsp honey or sugar

A bundle of herbs containing:
3 sprigs of thyme
2 sage leaves
2 bay leaves
1 strip orange or lemon rind (optional)

1. Place the olive oil in a large heavy-based pan, add the onions, celery and garlic and fry gently until soft but not coloured. Add the tomatoes and water. Tie the herbs together with a piece of kitchen string or in a small square of muslin and add them to the pan, along with the honey/sugar and salt. Simmer gently for 35 minutes until most of the liquid has evaporated. Taste and adjust the seasoning if necessary.
2. Remove the herb bundle. Allow the sauce to cool and pour into a blender. Whiz until completely smooth. Pour into a sterilised jar with a plastic lid. (Sterilise the jar by washing thoroughly and placing it in a preheated oven (160C/Gas 3) for 10 minutes.) Allow to cool slightly, then pour in the sauce, cover and keep in the fridge.

Use the sauce within 2 weeks.

Home-made tomato 'ketchup' – 2

450g tomatoes, skins and seeds removed and chopped
75g onion, finely chopped
1tsp tomato purée
4tbsp white vinegar
50g sugar
¼tsp salt
10 black peppercorns
2 cloves
1 bay leaf

1. Place the chopped tomatoes, tomato purée, and onion into a heavy-based saucepan. Tie the cloves, peppercorns and bay leaf in a piece of muslin and add to the pan. Cook gently for 20 minutes until the onion and tomato are soft. Remove the herb bundle.
2. Cool slightly and pour into a food processor or blender. Whiz until smooth. Strain through a sieve – try to push through as much of the pulp as possible.
3. Return to the saucepan and add the vinegar, sugar and salt. Simmer, stirring for about 15 minutes, until the mixture thickens and reaches a pouring consistency.
4. Pour into a sterilised jar with a plastic lid.

Use the sauce within 2 weeks (remember to label and date jars of the sauce so you know when it was made).

DESSERTS

Baked apples with figs
Serves 4

4 medium cooking apples
75g ready-to-eat dried figs
3tbsp water
2tsp butter or low-fat spread

1. Preheat the oven to 180C/Gas 4.
2. Remove the cores from the apples, and score round the centre of the apples. Chop the figs into small pieces and stuff the figs into the holes in the apples.
3. Place the apples in an ovenproof dish and top with a tiny knob of butter or low-fat spread. Pour the water into the dish. Cover the pan with foil and bake in the centre of the oven for 30 minutes.
4. Remove the foil and bake for a further 15 minutes or until the apples are soft.
5. Place the apples on serving plates, pour over any cooking juices. Serve with a tablespoon of natural yoghurt.

Variations
Fill the core of the apple with:

- Chopped dried apricots and raisins
- Crushed ginger biscuits made into a paste with a little honey
- Ground almonds and sultanas
- A little grated marzipan and some chopped dried apricots

Baked banana boats with fromage frais

These are really easy to make – they may not be much to look at, but the bananas go deliciously soft and creamy, and children like scooping out the sweet, mushy flesh.
Serves 4

4 medium bananas
2 small cartons fromage frais

1. Preheat the oven to 180C/Gas 4.
2. Put the bananas (with their skins on) on a baking tray and bake for 20 minutes until the skins are dark and the bananas soft to the touch.
3. Place the bananas on serving plates and slice each one in half lengthways. Serve with 2tbsp fromage frais.

Roast peaches with yoghurt

A perfect summer dessert, with hardly any added sugars
Serves 4

4 ripe peaches
2tbsp water
1tsp runny honey
2 small cartons yoghurt

1. Preheat the oven to 180C/Gas 4.
2. Wash the peaches and cut in half. Remove the stones.
3. Place the peaches in an ovenproof dish with their cut sides upwards. Warm the honey and water in a small ramekin in the microwave for 10 seconds, then pour the sauce over the peaches. Bake the peaches in the oven for 20 minutes or until they are tender.
4. Spoon half a carton of yoghurt onto each serving plate and arrange two peach halves on top. Pour over any cooking juices.

GLOSSARY

Accommodation/convergence failure – the inability of the eyes to move in towards the nose when looking at something close up, e.g. when reading

Alpha-linolenic acid – an omega-6 essential fatty acid

Amino acids – the 'building blocks' of protein

Antioxidants – nutrients that protect the body from oxidation damage (damage from harmful molecules called free radicals)

Arachidonic acid – a polyunsaturated fatty acid essential for growth

Artificial sweeteners – intensely sweet chemicals, with a fraction of the calories of sugar

Aspartame – also known as E951, the most infamous of the artificial sweeteners

Asperger's syndrome – a disorder in which the individual shows marked deficiencies in social skills, does not like change, often has obsessive routines and becomes preoccupied with particular subjects

Attention deficit disorder (ADD) – an inability to focus/concentrate on the job in hand, with a tendency to be easily distracted; tends to go hand in hand with ADHD and is a classic symptom of developmental delay

Attention deficit hyperactivity disorder (ADHD) – as for ADD above but with aspects of hyperactivity and impulsivity

Autism (true) – affects about 1 in 5,000 children, being four times more common in boys than girls; it has been thought for some time to be due to abnormal brain development and now would appear to be due to a lack of spindle cells; autistic children avoid eye contact, shun affection, do not understand other people's emotions/feelings, have problems making friends and cannot adjust to the rules of society

Autistic spectrum disorder (ASD) – affects 9 in 1,000 children – these children display autistic tendencies, and it may well prove to be an extreme form of developmental delay due to reduced numbers of spindle cells or greatly impaired spindle cell development

Benzoate – chemical used as a food preserver

Blood-sugar level – the level of glucose in the blood; has an impact on energy levels, concentration and mood

Bpoptosis – a term coined in 2005 by R Pauc to cover the period of time during which the second-wave/generation of human brain cells develop, migrate and make contact with other neurons

Brainstem – the part of the nervous system that joins the brain to the spinal cord; it contains many of the vital centres, vital because without them you die

Caffeine – a stimulant chemical found in coffee, tea, cola drinks and chocolate

Calories – also known as kcal, a measure of the energy in food

Carbohydrates – energy sources for the body, for example starches and sugars

Carcinogen – a substance thought to cause cancer

Central nervous system (CNS) – the brain and spinal cord

Cerebellar hemisphere – the cerebellum has a middle section with a large lobe on either side called a hemisphere

Cerebellum – literally 'little brain' that lives in the very back of the skull under the brain

Cerebral hemisphere – the name given to either side of the brain

Cholesterol (HDL) – the beneficial form of cholesterol, a chemical carried in the bloodstream; HDL cholesterol lowers the risk of heart attacks and stroke

Cholesterol (LDL) – the harmful form of cholesterol; having a high LDL cholesterol level increases your risk of clogged arteries, heart attacks and stroke

Chromosomal – to do with chromosomes, the threadlike structures found in the nucleus cells and that carry the genes

Congenital – present at birth

Diabetes – usually refers to diabetes mellitus, a disorder characterised by excessive urinary excretion; common types are type-1 juvenile diabetes, type-2 adult diabetes and gestational (occurring during pregnancy)

Disaccharide – a sugar made up of two single-sugar (monosaccharide) units; examples include sucrose (table sugar) and lactose (milk sugar)

Docosahexaenoic acid – an omega-3 essential fatty acid

Dressing dyspraxia – difficulty dressing

Dyslexia – a term used to cover a variety of learning difficulties

Dyspraxia – an inability to perform learned movements accurately; it can take many forms and has been found to be present in association with the other symptoms of developmental delay in over 90 per cent of children

Eicosanoids – short-lived hormone-like chemicals that perform many functions in the brain, including releasing neurotransmitters and regulating inflammation

Eicosapentaenoic acid – an omega-3 essential fatty acid

Empty calories – term used to describe foods that provide calories with little or no other nutritional benefit

Emulsifier – a substance that helps keep together other substances that normally would not stay together, for example oil and water

Equasym – a drug (active ingredient methylphenidate hydrochloride) used to 'treat' ADHD

Fibre – 'roughage', indigestible carbohydrate, found in wholegrains, fruit and vegetables, with benefits for the digestive and cardiovascular systems

Flavour/flavoured (on labels) – Only if the label says 'flavour*ed*' must it contain any of the food intended to provide the taste whatsoever; for example, orange flavour jelly doesn't have to contain orange

Foetal Alcohol Spectrum Disorder – a fairly recent term to cover both the physical and neurological effects to the foetus due to the maternal ingestion of alcohol during pregnancy

Foetal distress – when the foetal heartbeat rises or drops dramatically

Folic acid – one of the B-vitamins, also known as folate; helps the body to absorb nutrients effectively, and supports the immune system; during pregnancy, it also helps prevent neural tube defects in the developing baby

Free radicals – harmful molecules created by the oxidation process in the body, and implicated in health problems including clogged arteries, heart disease and cancer; neutralised by antioxidants

Functional foods – foods with added health benefits, such as eggs containing high levels of omega-3 fatty acids, or yoghurt drinks with added probiotics

Gamma-linoleic acid – an omega-6 essential fatty acid

Ghrelin – the so-called 'hunger hormone', which stimulates an increased desire for food

Glue ear – a condition when the middle ear is filled with a gluelike fluid instead of air

Glycaemic Index (GI) – a measure of food's impact on blood-sugar level

Glycaemic Load (GL) – an extension of the GI principle, which also takes into account the amount of carbohydrate in a food, and therefore probably gives a more 'practical' measure of its impact on blood sugar

Hormones – chemical messengers carried in the bloodstream

HUFAs – highly unsaturated fatty acids

Hydrogenated fats – artificial fats created by the food industry; source of harmful trans fats

Irritable Bowel Syndrome (IBS) – a multi-faceted disorder thought to be due to a disturbance in the interaction between the intestines, brain and the autonomic nervous system that alters the regulation of bowel function; it is characterised by abdominal pain or discomfort and is associated with a change in bowel pattern, such as loose or more frequent bowel movements, diarrhoea, and/or constipation

Lecithin – a fatlike substance called a phospholipid that is a fat emulsifier

Linoleic acid – an omega-6 essential fatty acid

Meconium – the first stool a baby passes

Methylphenidate hydrochloride – a central nervous system stimulant better known as Ritalin

Monosaccharide – a single-sugar unit, such as glucose or fructose

Monosodium glutamate (MSG) – a chemical flavour enhancer; has been implicated in symptoms including nausea and migraines in sensitive individuals

Monounsaturated fat – a 'healthy' class of fats, including olive oil

Motor planning – how the brain plans what it is it wants to do

Motor skills – the ability to carry out physical things you have learned to do

Myopic – being near-sighted

Neocortex – in terms of evolution, the newest parts of the brain

Neurologist – an expert in neurology

Neurology – the study of the nervous system

Neurons – nerves

Neurotransmitter – a chemical substance that passes messages from one nerve to the next

Nystagmus – the flickering of the eyes from side to side

Obsessive-compulsive disorder (OCD) – a disorder characterised by a recurrent urge to carry out ritualistic behaviour patterns, and a common symptom of developmental delay; to a certain extent we all have minor aspects of compulsive behaviour, only becoming a problem when it occurs to such a degree that it takes over a person's waking life

Omega-3 and omega-6 fatty acids – a group of essential fats, vital for good health, and especially healthy brain development and function

Partially hydrogenated fats – artificial fats created by the food industry; source of harmful trans fats

Phytochemicals – beneficial plant chemicals, found in foods such as fruit, vegetables, grains and pulses

Polysaccharide – a chain molecule composed of many monosaccharides (sugar units); examples include starch and cellulose

Prebiotic – a substance providing 'food' for the beneficial bacteria inhabiting the gut

Prefrontal cortex – a large area of brain (in humans) at the front of the brain

Probiotic – beneficial bacteria that inhabit the gut, promoting intestinal health and synthesising certain vitamins including vitamin K

Protein – food component vital for body growth and repair; good sources include lean meat, fish, eggs, dairy foods, nuts, seeds and pulses

PUFA – polyunsaturated fatty acid

Ritalin – the trade name for methylphenidate hydrochloride, a central-nervous-system stimulant used in the 'treatment' of ADHD

Saturated fat – fats found in animal products, and tropical oils (palm and coconut oil); implicated in increased risk of clogged arteries, heart disease and stroke

Serotonin – a neurotransmitter believed to play an important role in the regulation of mood, sleep, vomiting and appetite

Sodium chloride – the chemical name for salt

Spindle cells (von Economo cells) – special brain cells (nerves) that develop four months after birth in humans; they are only found in the brains of the great apes and humans; it is considered that these cells and the development of the prefrontal cortex (the front of the brain) is what makes us truly human

Statemented – the 1993 Education Act (UK) provided a code of practice giving guidance on how to identify and assess the special educational needs (SEN) of children; if it is felt that a child has SEN then a formal request can be made to have the child statemented, which if formally accepted should ensure the child's needs are met

Temporal sequencing – fitting events into a time frame

Tourette's syndrome – generally considered to be a condition in which a tic (involuntary movement) is associated with the sufferer swearing uncontrollably; however, minor aspects of it appear in so many children in the form of excessive blinking, grimacing or throat clearing for it to be considered a normal aspect of development

Trans fats – harmful fats produced by the hydrogenation process

Ventouse – an assisted birth using suction to pull the baby through the birth canal

Von Economo neurons – see 'spindle cells'

ABOUT THE AUTHORS

Robin Pauc DC DACNB FCC

Robin Pauc graduated from the Anglo-European College of Chiropractic in 1974. He studied neurology at post-graduate level in the Netherlands before qualifying in the USA. He was later awarded a professorship at the prestigious Carrick Institute at Cape Canaveral. He has lectured and taught clinical neurology internationally and has written several books including the bestselling *Is That My Child?* (UK) / *The Learning Disability Myth* (USA). He is currently the director of the Tinsley House Clinic UK.

Carina Norris MSc (Dist), RNutr

Nutrition consultant, author and journalist Carina Norris studied biology, followed by an MSc in Public Health Nutrition. She was the nutritionist for Channel 4's *Turn Back Your Body Clock* and has written several books on health and nutrition, including *You Are What You Eat: The Meal Planner That Will Change Your Life*, *Turn Back Your Body Clock*, *You Are What You Eat: Live Well, Live Longer*, and was the nutritionist and co-author of *Lorraine Kelly's Junk-Free Children's Eating Plan*. Carina is now working on a PhD on children's nutrient intakes. She has a passion to spread the word on healthy 21st-century living and help people de-junk their diets – the fun way.

INDEX